MW01233915

Praise For *Found a Job Yet?*

Judi is uniquely qualified to coach all of us and I am thankful she has shared her gifts with this book.

- **Peter Bourke**, author and speaker

A Better Way to Make a Living…and a Life

How many people do you know who are looking for a job? *Found a Job Yet?* is the book every family or friend of a job seeker should buy and read!

- **Brian Ray**, Founder and President of

Crossroads Career ® Network

As a Marriage and Family Therapist as well as a Career Counselor, my focus is the entire family's impact on job loss. I couldn't have written it better myself.

- **Debi C. Buckland**, MS, LMFT, LPC. Individual, Couple and Family Psychotherapist, Career Counselor

Unique among job search advice, no other book gives such an important voice to the unspoken need of jobseekers.

- **Susan Britton Whitcomb**, author of

The Christian's Career Journey

Judi Adams has a wonderful gift for bringing people into an understanding of the challenges, hopes, and encouragement needed by those in the process of searching for a job. She colorfully articulates the strain that a job search places on marriages, families, and other relationships and provides great wisdom through practical guidance and humor.

- **Trudy Simmons**, Licensed Clinical Pastoral Counselor, Founder of The Seven Bridges marriage program, and Speaker

FOUND A JOB YET

AND OTHER QUESTIONS NOT TO ASK!

THE PRACTICAL GUIDE FOR FAMILY AND FRIENDS

OF THOSE IN A JOB SEARCH

FOUND A JOB YET

AND OTHER QUESTIONS NOT TO ASK!

THE PRACTICAL GUIDE FOR FAMILY AND FRIENDS

OF THOSE IN A JOB SEARCH

THE BOOK EVERY JOB SEEKER

WISHES *you* HAD!

Judi Adams

FOUND A JOB YET? AND OTHER QUESTIONS <u>NOT</u> TO ASK!

Visit our website at www.FoundAJobYet.com for more information and additional resources.

Illustrations inspired by Sue Summerour
Illustrated by Judi Adams and Swapan Debnath, Copyright of RightChanges

Edited by Sandra Adams, Reba Shoulders, and Buck Trayser

Title ideas from Carole Hager, Melanie Trayser, and Debbie Baxter

Scripture taken from the HOLY BIBLE, NEW INTERNATIONAL VERSION Copyright © 1973, 1978, 1984 International Bible Society. Used by permission of Zondervan Bible Publishers.

The Six Steps and *Ask Others* are the copyright of Crossroads Career Services

<u>The Five Languages of Appreciation in the Workplace</u>, ©2011 by Gary Chapman and Paul E. White (Northfield Publishing)

<u>The Five Love Languages: The Secret to Love That Lasts</u>, ©2010 by Gary Chapman (Northfield Publishing)

"Me, Inc." is the copyright of Peter Bourke

FOREWORD

The rules of the hiring game have changed…forever. Knowing when, and more importantly, how to help a friend or loved one in their job search is both crucial and essential. Today, the job search takes longer than it has in decades. It gets lonely and discouraging out there. "Found a Job Yet" provides you with the knowledge, tools and methods that will powerfully support and leverage your "job seekers" efforts. Yes, the wrong words and actions can and will set them back. The right words and questions can help propel them past their competitors (the other job seekers) and help them turn their job search into a job found.

Skip Freeman, Recruiter and Author of *"Headhunter" Hiring Secrets- The Rules of the Hiring Game Have Changed… Forever!*

DEDICATION

This book is dedicated to the people in the lives of today's job seekers. Thank you! On behalf of your job seeker, thank you for caring enough to read this book. Whether you purchased this book yourself or received it from a job seeker, it indicates that you are an important person in the life of someone who is in a job transition and they need and want your support.

To all job seekers of today: we are here for you.

ACKNOWLEDGEMENT

Special thanks go to the people who made the birth of this book possible.

To **Brian and Kristy Ray** of Crossroads Career Services for creating the Crossroads program. You were there for me when I was in my job search and helped light my passion for those in job transitions. Thank you, too, Brian for encouraging me to get *Found a Job Yet? And Other Questions <u>Not</u> to Ask!* out into the market to fill the need that exists.

To the **volunteers of Crossroads Career Network (CCN)** across the country who selflessly help job seekers every day through their job transition. To **Peter Bourke** who works with CCN and launched the job networking and support group C3G that provides help and encouragement to the participants.

To **Buck Trayser** of Mt. Paran Crossroads and fellow techie who served as a sounding board for ideas and approaches, checked the statistics that I quote, and encouraged me to borrow from his storehouse of materials. To the **CCN team at Dunwoody Baptist** who helped me in my job search.

To my friend **Reba Shoulders** who first mentioned Crossroads to me, who has seen me through so many chapters of my life, and then, as an experienced writer, helped with editing this book. To **Scott Becker** who is like a brother and gave of his time and talent to help with editing.

To my cousin **Sue Summerour** who used her artistic talents to capture my analogies so they could be communicated to Swapan.

To **my clients** who held me accountable for writing and completing this book while I was holding them accountable in their transition. They will remain nameless out of professional discretion but you know who you are. Thank you for your encouragement. A special thank you to **the spouses of my clients** who met with me and shared their struggles, needs, ideas, and their encouragement for this book.

To the **job seekers** who submitted ideas and stories used in this book for the benefit of others. It is through this book I give you a voice that you may have felt you did not have with those closest to you. The stories you shared are very much appreciated.

To my professional associates who refer clients to me because they care for them. **Cathryn Marshall Outlaw, Curt Engelmann, and others** too many to name, thank you.

To **Mimi Nguyen** who gave generously to me when I was in my job search and through the launch of my business. Now your generosity is being read about by many. Thank you.

To **Mrs. Cathy Teaford Williams,** my high school English teacher who introduced me to the power of analogies and to **Marcia Sandula** who coached me in improving my writing.

To my amazing sister **Sandra Adams.** You are my life and a daily inspiration to me.

And of course to **my heavenly Father** who gave me the passion for and the honor of serving Him in this way. It is my prayer that every job seeker finds a job they love as much as I love this one.

Table of Contents

Introduction

Found a Job Yet? And Other Questions <u>Not</u> to Ask! is the first job search book of its kind on the market. This book is not addressed to job seekers. Instead, this book is written for friends, family, and spouses of job seekers.

To Friends, Spouses, Parents, and Other Family Members:

You want to help your job seeker but you may not know where to start or, with the kindest intentions, you may be doing the wrong things. Your job seeker wants your help but may not know how to ask you or does not understand themself how you can be of assistance. This guide answers those questions.

You play an important role in the life of the job seeker and in their success. Your help is needed to create a positive environment and provide much needed assistance. On behalf of the job seeker in your life, thank you for caring and wanting to help. Your encouragement and support will help them stay motivated so they can take the right steps and find their next job.

To Job Seekers:

Consider sharing *Found a Job Yet? And Other Questions Not to Ask!* with the people in your life so they know how to be supportive of you during your search. They want to help; they may not know what to do or how to give you the support you need and want.

When sharing the book with people in your support group, consider saying that you really appreciate them and all they have done (give specific examples). Share with them that you have had a hard time putting into words what it has been like going through the job search this time. Ask them if they will do you a favor by reading this book. Then you can use it as a starting point for your conversation about what you have been going through.

Updates to *Found a Job Yet? And Other Questions <u>Not</u> to Ask!*

We want to give you the latest information. Life is changing faster than ever before in history. If you do not believe it, buy a technical device such as a computer or cell phone. By the time you get it home, there is a newer model on the market with more functions and it costs less than what you paid. The job market is continually changing as well. Even as this book was being written I had to go back and update it as changes occurred.

At the end of this book, I provide a link to a website with the changes that occurred since *Found a Job Yet?* was initially published so you have the latest information.

Let's get started...

How to Use This Guide

As a member of your job seeker's support team, nothing feels as helpless as seeing them struggle in the job search and wanting to help but not knowing where to begin. Just as bad is realizing that what you are doing is not working. This is a common theme in my conversations with family members that I had the pleasure to meet at speaking engagements and in my one-on-one coaching practice. In the case of spouses, not only do you have the feeling of helplessness, but you are also directly affected by the job transition.

Knowledge is strength. *Found a Job Yet?* will help familiarize you with the new job market and ideas on how to (and how not to) be supportive of the job seeker.

Found a Job Yet? was written to be read in its entirety first. You can then use sections as a reference to develop an action plan and to serve as a regular reminder of things to do and say, and what *not* to do and say.

Where to Start

The job market has changed drastically over the past decade and even more so in the past few years. The job seeker cannot successfully navigate in the job market unless they understand how it has changed and what they need to do to be successful. As their support system, the first thing you need to do is understand how the job market has changed so you know what they are going through. We will begin by examining the new realities of the job market: the bad and the good news.

The next things you will want to understand are the steps that are required to find a job. The Six Steps – How to Walk Through a Crossroads In Your Career are from the Crossroads Career Services program and are Attitude, Aptitude, Altitude, Search, Sort, and Select. The Steps will be covered in more detail in later chapters. The first three Steps should be taken even before the job seeker updates their résumé. As we review the Steps, we will not get into the details needed by the job seeker; that is not the purpose for this book. This book will provide enough information for you to understand what is required so you can fulfill your role in helping your job seeker.

We will look at the various approaches for finding a job and the success rates associated with each.

There is a separate chapter dedicated to spouses of job seekers.

You will hear directly from job seekers. Their comments are in response to the following questions:

- What is the best thing anyone did for you while you were in your job search?

- What is the worst thing?

- What do you wish they had done?

At the end of most chapters, there is a separate section titled "Believer's Bonus" that contains faith-based materials related to that topic.

NOTE: Instead of contorting a sentence to eliminate the need to specify a gender specific pronoun, shifting between using the male and female pronouns in my examples, or saying "he/she" repeatedly, I have chosen to use "they", "their", and

"them" as singular, non-gender specific pronouns as well as

plural pronouns.

Part I

The New Realities

Chapter 1

Realities of Today's Job Market

> *"I've a feeling we're not in Kansas anymore"*
> - Dorothy (Wizard of Oz, 1939)

Nothing feels as helpless as wanting to help a loved one in a job search and not knowing where to begin. Knowledge is power.

The very first things you, as the support person for your job seeker, need to know are the new realities of the job market. If you are of the Baby Boomer generation or older, or have not been in a job search recently, you will be shocked by how much the job market has changed. The job seeker did not do anything to create this change. It happened and, to be successful, the job seeker must adapt to the new job market.

Without understanding the reality that the job seeker is facing, you cannot really be supportive. Offering advice based on a past reality is outdated and ineffectual. By understanding the realities of the new job market you will better appreciate what your job seeker is going through and know what you are talking about when discussing the job search with them.

The Realities of the New Job Market

Not only has the whole job market changed, the approach for successfully finding a job has changed as well.

Those of you who have read any of my other materials or heard me speak know I use a *lot* of analogies. A good analogy for not knowing the realities of the new job market is like walking into a pitch black warehouse and being told you have to walk to the other side. It is so dark in the warehouse that you cannot see your hand in front of your face; you cannot see where you need to go or the obstacles that are in the way. You can work as hard as you can, but without knowing where the exit is, you have no way to know if you are making progress. You may just be walking in circles.

Knowing the realities of the new job market is like turning the lights on in the warehouse (Illustration 1.1). Even though it is not a pretty place to be and you do not want to spend a lot of time there, you can see where you need to go, what obstacles are in the way, how to get around them, and see the progress you are making.

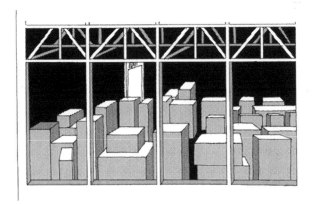

1.1 The Warehouse: Realities of the New Job Market

Your job seeker needs to understand these realities and so do you. Let us turn the lights on and see what your job seeker is facing. We will start with how the job market has changed. (Illustration 1.2 – 1.5.)

The Job Market of *Yesteryear*

1.2 The Rotary Dial Phone - The Job Market of Yesteryear

In my grandfather's home there was one phone. It was a very heavy, rotary dial phone, and was wired into the wall. Since there was only one phone in most homes it was usually located in a central location such as the bottom of the stairs in a two story house or in the kitchen. That is the analogy of the job market of *yesteryear*.

- In that job market, people had one, maybe two jobs or careers in a lifetime. My mom's father was a farmer all his life; my dad's father was a carpenter; my father was career Navy. For people who worked in manufacturing plants, glass factories, and others local industries generations of families worked the same job at the same company. Not only is that the only job they have ever known, that is the only job their fathers, and their fathers' fathers, have even known.

- Only poor performers were laid off, sometimes not even them. Companies took care of their employees; sometimes poor performers were moved into non-critical areas instead of being fired because they were considered family.

- If a résumé was even needed to find a job, it was a generic chronological résumé that was used for any position or industry. The job seeker would have one version printed and copies generated by a professional printer on colored or special résumé paper.

- Available jobs were posted in the newspaper or on signs in the shop window. Recruiters were the only other source of job leads.

- References were not required because people knew each other.

- Hobbies and outside interests were listed on the résumé because companies wanted to hire well rounded people who would be with them their entire career.

- All functions were done within the company and very little work was outsourced. The term offshoring had not yet been coined [1-1] although there were campaigns to "Buy American" by labeling items as "Made in the U.S.A." [1-2]

- People worked at the same company their entire career, retired with a gold watch, pension, and full benefits.

- Big companies meant stability. Think back to the quote, "As GM goes, so goes the nation". [1-3]

- If you did not have a job, you were a deadbeat; it was because you did not want to work.

That was the job market of *yesteryear*.

The Job Market of *Yesterday*

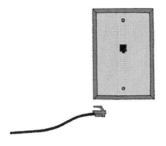

1.3 The Modular Phone - The Job Market of Yesterday

The home phone moved from the rotary dial phone to touchtone modular phones. Every home was built with a number of modular plugs in almost every room. It was not unusual for there to be several phones throughout the home. Although the phone was still plugged into the wall, you could easily unplug it and plug it in somewhere else and fully expect it to work just as well there.

That is the analogy for the job market of *yesterday*.

- People were still employees of companies (whether corporations, government agencies, or non-profits), which is represented by plugging the phone into the wall. However, people would change careers, jobs, and companies. In fact, people averaged up to 13 jobs and up to 4 careers in a lifetime. [1-4] Still, longevity was admired and anyone who left a company after only a few years were considered "a job hopper", which was a derogatory term.

- In most industries, companies did away with pensions. Even in industries known for unions and pensions, changes were made to eliminate pension plans for future generations. [1-5] In more recent times, companies have reduced or eliminated 401(k) company contributions. [1-6]

- With ready access to home computers and printers, résumés were customized for each position. Many résumés were still chronological and began with a career objective that stated what the job seeker wanted. Special or colored paper was no longer used.

- Available jobs were sometimes still listed in the help want ad section of the newspaper, but with the advent of online job boards, newspapers were used less often to post positions. Recruiters were receiving less work orders as companies started saving money by posting their jobs on the online job boards or their own company web sites.

- References were available upon request.

- People started living longer and wanted to keep active and maintain a certain standard of living. People therefore planned to work until they were no longer able to work, although they might change what they were doing.

- Non-core business functions were outsourced and in some cases even certain core business functions were.

- Smaller companies were more agile and able to change as technology and the world changed. Therefore, smaller companies offered more stability and larger companies were "right-sizing" to become competitive.

Although this might sound familiar to most of today's workers, that is the job market of *yesterday*.

Today's Job Market

1.4 The Cell Phone - The Job Market of Today

Today's job market is like today's home phones. Many people are getting away from having a home phone that plugs into a wall and are using their cell phone or the Internet (Voice over IP) for all voice conversations.

- Where companies used to have a majority of full-time workers, today companies are looking at a contingent and part-time work force. This trend is exemplified in the new terminology "on-demand workforce" and "contingent talent" or just "CT". People more and more will be contracting to and working *with* but not

working *for* a company. [1-7]

- People will be responsible for their own benefits.

    o   With the uncertainty of Social Security and lack of

    pension plans, people will be responsible for

    providing for their own retirement. Even if a

    company offers a 401(k) match, the employee may

    not be at the company long enough to be vested

    in the company's contribution.

    o   Recent graduates are being advised to get their

    own personal health and term life insurance so it

    moves with them unlike group policies. (This also

    eliminates the concern about later needing to

    qualify once pre-existing conditions come into

    play.)

- Job security from a company is not a certainty anymore.

Today, positions are eliminated regardless of employee

performance. Companies no longer offer job security, nor

can they with the changes happening in the world and within business. We do not get our signal (job security) from plugging into a wall (company) but from our network. Job security will come from within the person, knowing what they have to offer, developing an active and ongoing network, keeping their skills and experiences are kept in demand. Just as importantly, a job seeker must be able to communicate the relevancy of these skills and experiences into value for the company.

Peter Bourke says in his book *A Better Way to Make a Living and a Life - Thriving in the New World of Work,* "...the biggest change in the new world of work has to do with the worker's attitude." Peter goes on to say, "…workers have realized it is not always prudent to be entirely reliant on just one employer. Perhaps the organization most worthy of our long term commitment is one called Me, Inc."

Job security now comes from something we control. By maintaining our marketability, keeping up our skills, and expanding our experience, we stay in demand. Job security is not based on a company which may be bought out, may fold, or outsource job functions.

- Today companies outsource many aspects of the work, providing just oversight.

- Résumé formats have changed. Since each résumé only receives 8 – 12 seconds of a glance when candidates are screened, the résumé format has moved from chronological to the combination résumé. The résumé should begin with a career summary instead of an objective since companies care less about what the candidate wants and more about what the candidate can do for them.

- Résumés are only one piece, and the least used, of the marketing materials required by a job seeker today. In

Chapter 6, we will highlight all of the materials a job seeker now needs in their search for a job.

- Social networking is now an essential part of the job seeker's marketing collateral. LinkedIn is a required component and the use of Twitter is growing. Although Facebook remains mostly social in nature, it plays a role in the job search. Blogging can even be used as a tool for the job search. [1-8]

- Providing references is required, and has been for a while. No mention of references is made on the résumé.

- There is no shame in being temporarily unemployed. It is like the transition from one grade in school to another. It is truly just a point of transition; we just need to understand that it will be the new norm and prepare for it.

That is the job market of *today*.

Here is a table that compares the job markets of yesteryear, yesterday, and today.

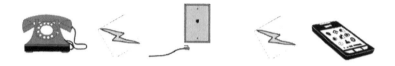

Yesteryear Rotary Dial Phone	Yesterday Modular Phone	Today Cell Phone
1-2 careers and jobs in a lifetime	13 + jobs and 4 careers in a lifetime	Work with, not for, multiple companies
Retirement at 65 with a gold watch, pension, and benefits	May not retire, just change the form of work; no pension, 401(k) company contribution being cut back or eliminated	Responsible for own retirement and benefits
Full-time employees and all services done in house	Outsource non-core functions; part time or contract employees to handle the up's and down's of work	Not an employee; provide expertise to companies as needed
Big companies meant stability and job security	Smaller companies mean stability	Job security is a personal responsibility

1.5 - Comparison of the Job Markets

Causes of the New Job Market

Like with the evolution of the home phone, we did not get a vote in how the job market changed. So what caused this new market? Many things contributed to reshaping the job market to what it is today.

Dot-com and Telecom Busts

In the late 1990's and until March 2000, the economy was growing at a rapid rate, too rapid for some sectors, and like a bubble it burst. Many companies that were created during the boom are now bust. Some of the biggest busts occurred in the telecom and IT (.com) sectors and in 2007 the banking and housing sectors. [1-9]

Exporting and Offshoring of Jobs

Since 1995, U.S. firms sent manufacturing jobs to other countries. Since then call centers and technology jobs were off-shored. Now U.S. firms are sending technical writing, engineering, and other job functions to other countries. The only jobs that cannot be offshored are those that require a physical presence. [1-10]

Gas Prices

In 2008, when gas priced reached a new record in the U.S., I paid $4.29 a gallon for regular gas in Georgia where the prices were lower than many other areas of the country. Today, the price of gas is reaching those levels again. As gas prices rise, companies with products and services not directly tied to the price of gas are being negatively impacted as families are making the tough decisions about where they spend their money.

Housing Market

The downturn in the housing market has impacted many other sectors including construction, real estate, property managers, and mortgage companies.

Banking

Georgia, where I live, has been leading the nation in the number of closed banks. Every week we read in the business paper about the next group of banks that failed. [1-11]

Auto Industries

I was working in the auto industry when it was floundering in 2008. Although the auto industry has recovered some, there are makes of cars we will never see again.

Travel and Hospitality Industry

The attacks on 9/11 had a direct impact on the travel and hospitality industries because air travel was shut down in the U.S. for days and some airlines never recovered. Since then, other events, such as the new security measures and diseases, have negatively

impacted these industries. [1-12]

Corporate Mergers

The term "merger" does not sound so scary until

you realize that by merging, there is an automatic

redundancy of positions and "merger" usually means

people will be laid off.

Stock Market "Correction" and the Recession

In 2000, the U.S. and other countries went

through a stock market "correction" and in 2007 we

started to experience a full blown recession. Although, as

of the writing of this book, we have, by definition, come

out of the recession, so far it has been a jobless recovery,

the phenomenon where the overall economy experiences

growth while maintaining or decreasing its level of employment. [1-13]

War and Conflicts

Following the attacks of 9/11, the U.S. went to war and we are still in conflict. Countries in the Middle East are going through unrest or worse. At a minimum, the uncertainty of these events impacts consumer confidence, which negatively impacts the economy and, in turn, the job market.

Natural Disasters

In recent times, major natural disasters including earthquakes, tsunamis, volcanic eruptions, floods, droughts, fires, and tornadoes have impacted local businesses and the global economy, and in turn, the job market.

In 2011, Japan's earthquake and resulting tsunami triggered damage to the Fukushima Daiichi power plant, causing concerns about how far reaching the resulting damage will be. This same natural disaster has impacted the supply of parts for the auto industry. [1-14]

Man-Made Disasters

The U.S. businesses along the Gulf of Mexico experienced a horrible economic impact when the BP oil spill occurred in 2010 and became the worst oil spill in U.S. History. [1-15]

Global Diseases

I was watching the job market in 2003 when the disease Severe Acute Respiratory Syndrome (SARS) hit. I was surprised to read that SARS hurt the international travel industry as badly if not worse than the attacks of 9/11 and war combined. [1-16] That makes sense though.

People do not want to be in the body of the plane, which is like an enclosed tube, breathing the same air as someone who is critically ill and contagious.

It is no surprise then that when in 2003 the H1N1 virus (also known as the swine flu) hit in the summer time (which is not normal for flu) and was impacting a sector of the population not normally at risk (the young); people did not believe that it was just a strain of flu. People cut back on their unnecessary plane travel. Delta and the airline then named AirTran (which later merged with Southwest Airlines) attributed the drop in traffic not only to the recession but the concern over H1N1 as well.

1-17

The Bad News

The results of these events are evident in the job market. Let us first look at the bad news.

Layoff of Highly Skilled Employees

In my grandfather's time, if you did not have a job, you were a deadbeat. Today, thousands of highly skilled professionals are looking for work. You could form a company with the talent that exists in most any room where job seekers congregate.

It now takes longer to find a job than ever before. Higher level positions take even longer than others. Even a mid-level job can take months to land. [1-18]

> "It's a recession when your neighbor loses his job; it's a depression when you lose yours."
> Harry S. Truman, in Observer,
> April 13, 1958
> 33rd President of the U.S.

Unprecedented Unemployment

The biggest surprise to me, in my own job search in 2002, was to find out the unemployment number does not reflect the true state of affairs. When you hear the high unemployment number, realize it is greatly understated. The Department of Labor (DOL) and the Bureau of Labor Statistics measure the number of unemployed by taking a monthly sample survey called the Current Population Survey (CPS). There are 60,000 households in the sample survey for a four month period. This number is referred to as the U-3. [1-19]

Even if the DOL used for the unemployment count the number of people receiving an unemployment check, it would not include the following categories of people:

- Recent graduates
- People recently laid off but still receiving severance pay
- People who did not apply for unemployment out of some illogical sense of shame (it is unemployment *insurance*

and in most states was paid for on their behalf by their former employer; it is not charity). [1-20]

- Contractors who are between contracts

- The self-employed whose businesses failed

- Those who have been unemployed for so long that they have exhausted their unemployment benefits

- Job seekers who have given up looking, referred to as discouraged workers

- People who have accepted a part-time or "bridge" job and are still looking for work

- People who are coming out of retirement and looking for work to maintain a certain standard of living

- People re-entering the workforce after taking time out to raise a family

The economy and resulting Job Market that started in December 2007 is referred to as the Great Recession.

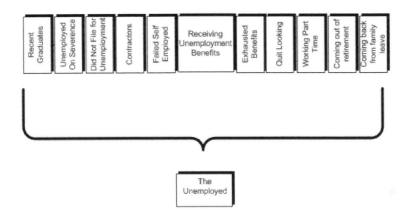

1.6 - Picture of the Real Unemployment Number

When the unemployment number goes down, there is some hope that it is because there are more jobs. There is just as strong of a chance that people have moved into one of the other unemployed categories.

The Bureau of Labor Statistics (www.bls.gov) tries to extrapolate the "real" unemployment number. They refer to this number as the U-6. [1-21]

Reluctance to Spend

Even those who are employed are reluctant to spend money because their house value is not what it used to be, their 401(k) is not what it needs to be, gas prices are going up, and their neighbor lost their job and they could be next. This reluctance to spend, though, stalls the economy resulting in more closed businesses and therefore more unemployment.

Employed People are Unhappy in Their Current Jobs

In addition to the people who are currently in a transition, a great number of people (estimated between 40% and 50% [1-22], sometimes quoted as high as 85%) who are working are not happy in those jobs and are looking to change. Because of the downsizing, they have to do more work, and some managers are taking advantage of the economy to overwork and underappreciate their employees. They are ready to leave their jobs once the economy gets better. This is known as "voluntary attrition".

Moving in with Family

People of all ages are moving in with family members to save money. Children, regardless of age, are moving in with their parents, and some parents are moving in with their adult children.

Delayed Retirement

Natural attrition occurs when a generation of people reaches the age of retirement, freeing up jobs for the next generation. This natural attrition is not happening today at the normal rate. [1-23] The money is not there to retire because their house values are not what they used to be and retirement nest eggs are not what they need to be to support the desired lifestyle. Making the unemployment problem worse is that some people who were retired are coming out of retirement because their investments (house and stocks) have lost value or their retirement benefits have been taken away and they must now work to cover their living expenses. With entire classes of students graduating each semester and joining the workforce, we are encountering compression, where more and more people are vying for the same jobs.

Companies are not Knocking on Job Seekers' Doors and Recruiters are not Returning All Phone Calls

Before the market changed, companies actively pursued people with certain skills; that has changed. Following the dot-com bust in 2000, the phones of Information Technology workers did not ring like they used to. This is true for other industries as well.

For years, recruiters were a valuable resource for finding a job. That was true at least until the invention of internet job boards. Recruiters are working a smaller number of job orders while they are deluged with résumés and phone calls from job seekers. Recruiters just cannot return everyone's phone calls.

Understand as well that it is not the recruiter's job to find jobs for job seekers. Recruiters are paid by companies to find the right candidate.

A fundamental truth about today's job market is that each person's job is likely not their last. Everyone will be on the job market again at some point. [1-24]

> *[From a friend of a job seeker] I will admit at first I did not believe there was a recession because it had not impacted me personally at all.*
>
> - Theresa W.

This is a defining moment for the members of this job market. When I share this information with audiences, you can see their faces fall. Hold on. That is the bad news about the job market. Now for the good news and there is good news.

The Good News

Every day people are finding work, and it is work they enjoy. In a recent Bureau of Labor Statistics Job Openings and Labor Turnover (JOLT) report, four million people are being hired every month and three million positions are still unfulfilled. [1-25]

Each job seeker is unique and has their own set of skills and abilities. They will get a job if they do the following:

- Know the realities of the new job market and how to navigate in it

- Choose a positive attitude

- Develop a set of the new powerful marketing collateral highlighting prior accomplishments

- Follow the Six Steps

- Are prepared

Currently, with the grace of God, 100% of the clients who have completed my company's personal coaching program are now employed in jobs they wanted. A number of my clients found jobs even before completing the program but continued in the program because they know they will be on the job market again.

This is the reality of the new job market.

Next we will look at the Six Steps that are required to find a job. Remember, updating the résumé is NOT the first step; it is not even in the first three steps.

Chapter Summary

Job seekers cannot effectively navigate in the new job market without understanding it. You need to understand it, too, if you want to be supportive.

Believer's Bonus

Even the scriptures say it is wise to learn about the new job market.

Let the wise listen and add to their learning, and let the discerning get guidance...

- Proverbs 1:5

The discerning heart seeks knowledge, but the mouth of a fool feeds on folly.

– Proverbs 15:14

A fool finds no pleasure in understanding but delights in airing his own opinions.

– Proverbs 18:2

By wisdom a house is built, and through understanding it is established; through knowledge its rooms are filled with rare and beautiful treasures. A wise man has great power, and a man of knowledge increases strength.

– Proverbs 24:3-5

A man who loves wisdom brings joy to his father.

– Proverbs 29:3

And it could happen to you.

Do not boast about tomorrow for you do not know what a day may bring forth.

– Proverbs 27:1

Do not be like the Pharisee that prayed about himself: "God I thank you that I am not like other men".

– Luke 18:11

Life is full of uncertainty and we often experience more of God in the midst of uncertainty; our faith is strengthened by experiencing God's presence.

"My Father is always at his work to this very day, and I, too, am working."

– John 5:17

Chapter 2

Introduction to the Six Steps of the Job Search

For many job seekers, when they learn that they are being "right-sized" or when they get fed up at work and decide to leave, their first impulse is to update their résumés with their most current work history and start applying online. That is a natural reaction.

Although that is the initial inclination, it is not the first step a job seeker should take. According to Crossroads Career Services, and common logic as you will see, there are six steps to the job search and updating the résumé is not Step 1; it does not even take place until after Step 3.

Missing the first three steps of the job search will sabotage the job search effort. I will say that again: if job seekers miss the first three steps, they are sabotaging their own job search efforts.

The first three steps of the job search are like the legs of a three-legged stool (Illustration 2.1). The stool is not worth very much without all three legs; you would not think about standing on it if one leg was missing. In the same way, job seekers cannot afford to skip the first three steps.

2.1 The Three-Legged Stool – The First Three Steps of the Job Search

Let us look at Crossroads Career Services Six Steps ™.

2.2 Crossroads Career Services Six Steps of the Job Search

I need to say one thing first. Have patience with the

process and celebrate progress. The hardest part sometimes, for

everyone involved, is that until there are marketing materials

developed and applications being submitted, it feels there is

nothing substantial being done. In the same way when building

a home, there is not a lot of excitement until the walls go up. You know however, that it is the foundation that provides the structure a firm base. In the same way, the first three steps are the foundation to the job search.

Step 1 is **Attitude**. If the job seeker has a bad attitude, it will show in their body language, their word choices, or in the energy they need to do the job search. Job seekers need to process the loss and choose a good attitude in order to be successful in the job search.

Step 2 is **Aptitude**. You cannot sell a product unless you know how it works and what makes it better than the competition's. The same is true for job seekers. They must know their product – the skills, abilities, and accomplishments that make them better than their competition. They must be able to answer the interviewer's question "Why should we hire you?" The answer "I need a job" will not get them the job.

Step 3 is **Altitude**. This is the step when job seekers define where they want to work and who is hiring. This is also the step when they define all of their requirements (for example salary, geography). They have to know what they want in order to get it.

Once job seekers have chosen a positive attitude, know their competitive advantages, and know the companies they are targeting, they can then update their marketing materials. The term marketing material is used for the résumé and other items needed for the job search because the job seeker is "selling" their skills and experience just like a salesperson sells a product. They need to target their marketing materials and include their competitive advantage or else their marketing materials will fall flat.

In today's job search, the résumé is not the only article of the job seeker's marketing collateral. There are many more marketing materials required than ever before and the résumé may be the least used of them. Chapter 6 will cover the marketing materials required, at a minimum, in a job search in today's job market.

Now that job seekers have their marketing materials completed, they begin Step 4 the **Search**. In Chapter 7 we examine the various approaches to searching for a job and the success rates for each.

Step 5 is **Sort** which is another term for interview.

Step 6 is **Select** which means selecting the right opportunity.

The dashed line in illustration 2.2 means the next job is probably not the last. The reality of the job market is that job seekers will be on the job market again, and there are action items they must take while employed to make the next transition shorter and easier. Everyone who is still in the workforce should consider taking these actions as well.

Now that we have introduced you to the Six Steps, let us look at each one in detail. After we go through all Six Steps, we will examine what you can do to help your job seeker with their job search.

Chapter 3

Attitude

The Most Important Step

Attitude is the first and most important step. When a person loses their job, feelings are raw; it is one of life's biggest stressors. Losing a job attacks the person's sense of self, their ability to provide for their basic needs, and they have lost the purpose and structure to their days that a job provides. Too often our jobs define us; it reinforces our worth to our family and to others.

If the job seeker does not process their emotions, it will show in their body language, word choice, or the energy needed to do the job search.

Body Language

Look at Illustration 3.1. Although she is saying, "I'm thrilled to be here" her body language indicates otherwise. People trust a person's body language over the words spoken.

The same is true of your job seeker. Your job seeker can be saying all of the right things; they could have given the best answer to the interview question than any other candidate. However, if the body language is saying "do not hire me" due to lack of confidence (shoulders slumped, head lowered) or anger (defiant stance, set jaw), then the hiring manager will believe the body language over the words spoken and move on to the next candidate.

3.1 A Bad Attitude

Word Choice

Did you know the words "but" and "why" have a negative connotation? The word "but" in a sentence negates everything said before it. "I want to give you an increase but..." means you are probably not getting the increase.

The word "why" is associated with having to justify oneself. "Why did you do that?" sounds a lot more accusatory than the question "What was the driving thought behind that decision?" The "what" question gets to the same answer and puts the emphasis on the reasoning behind the action rather than on the person.

"Just" is another word that is added before a job description to minimize the importance of the job. It irritates me when I hear someone say, "I was just an admin". Just? I ask you, how could we function in the business world without administrative assistants? I know it is not a world I would want to live in.

If the job seeker does not address attitude, they may use words that minimize themselves or make them come off as negative.

Energy to do the Search

No one that I have met has said looking for a job is fun; that is because it is not. So imagine starting out with a negative attitude. When the job seeker is not looking forward to getting out of the bed, they will not feel like doing the things they need to do that may be outside of their comfort zone, like attending networking events.

So what does the job seeker need to do to choose a positive attitude?

Process the Loss

Job seekers must give themselves time and permission to process the loss. If they do not heal from the loss, it will come out at the most inopportune time, like in the middle of a job interview.

We are all human and in order to heal from a loss, we must go through the five stages of grieving. According to Elizabeth Kübler -Ross and David Kessler's book *On Grief and Grieving*, these steps include denial, depression, anger, bargaining, and the final step acceptance. [3-1] People go through these steps in different orders and take a different amount of time in the various stages. The important thing is that job seekers give themselves permission and take the time to grieve to get to the stage of acceptance.

Accept the Opportunity

Once the job seeker has processed the loss, attitude is then a choice. Job seekers need to choose a great attitude and get to the point where they are excited about the new opportunity before them. This may be just the event in their life that allows them to seek the job they have always wanted.

What I know is that there is a plan for your job seeker, one that will prosper them and not harm them, one that will give them hope and a future. Wow! That is a great plan and the one they want. It is what you want for your job seeker too.

Pressure Points

During the job search, finding a job is not their only concern. Job seekers are also concerned with keeping the roof over their head, the car in the driveway, and food on the table.

Job seekers may need help with these pressure points and others as well.

See Illustration 3.2 and imagine if that was your home. Would you hesitate to call the fire department if your house was on fire? I am fairly sure you said "no". It would be absurd to stand there and watch your house burn down when, by a single phone call, you could get the help you need to save your house.

3.2 - Would You Hesitate to Call 911 if This Was Your House?

In this simple example we realize there are times in our lives when we need to ask others for help. Even if you were a professional fireman, you would not hesitate to call 911 if your house was on fire. [3-2] You would want the help of other firemen, and the fire hose is a lot more effective than a garden hose for putting out a fire. So even if you are skilled enough to handle issues, there are times you, like all of us, need the help of others.

Many of us call 411 for directory assistance (or look the number up on the Internet). [3-3] In the U.S. and Canada, the phone number 511 is available in most areas for traffic information. [3-4] The number 211 is a dedicated number in the U.S. and Canada. You may or may not have heard of. It is the number set aside for providing health and human service information and referral. [3-5] The wonderful people answering the calls to 211 know of numerous programs and services that provide critical information on, and assistance with consumer credit issues, the latest mortgage assistance programs, food banks, clothes closets, and sources of emotional support, and more. Many of these services are free or available on a sliding scale.

I found out about the 211 number when I talked to the Benevolence Director at my church. My church wanted to help people in our community and it would have taken a monumental effort to notify everyone in our community on a regular basis about the services we wanted to provide. We tapped into the 211 network because they do a fabulous job of coordinating these services.

Unemployment Insurance

Unemployment insurance is just that, insurance. [3-6] We pay for house and car insurance so if something drastic occurs, the insurance is there to cover the costs of repairs or replacement. If the car is totaled we would not hesitate to file a car insurance claim; after all, that is the reason we pay the premiums.

People who have lost their jobs should not feel bad about filing an unemployed insurance claim. In most of the states in the U.S., companies pay the premiums for the employee's unemployment insurance on behalf of the employee. In a few states the employee contributes to these premiums.

Unemployment insurance is there for people who have worked hard and are transitioning between jobs.

All job seekers should contact the Department of Labor office to see if they qualify for unemployment benefits and qualified job seekers should apply for unemployment immediately. Each state has its own guidelines but there is usually a waiting period. If the job seeker is receiving a severance they should go ahead and file; they may not collect until the severance ends.

A Bridge Job

A "bridge job" is a job to bring in some money while the job seeker continues searching for the job they want. In some cases, the bridge job may not be a job that utilizes the job seeker's full skills and abilities. There is no shame in securing a bridge job; honest work is honest work. There are, however, several misconceptions about a bridge job.

1) One misconception is that the bridge job is easier to find; in fact it can be harder to find.

   - Hiring managers understand that job seekers who take a bridge job will not stay around for long. Once the right job comes along or the economy picks up, the job seeker will probably leave. Hiring managers do not want to bring someone on board just to have the person leave, requiring the company to go through the work and expense of hiring another person after only a short period of time.

   - There are people who aspire to have these jobs. Although you might think hiring managers would be thrilled to have so much talent for such little money, hiring managers would rather hire someone who has passion for the job than someone who is settling.

2) Another misconception of the bridge job is that once the job seeker has the bridge job, it will take the pressure off and make finding the real job easier.

- Self-esteem and self-confidence do not increase when job seekers are working in jobs that do not provide the pay, benefits, or challenge based on their skills and abilities. Taking a job that does not fulfill or challenge them can have a negative impact on attitude, which will affect the chances of future success.

- The job search process is a full-time job. Having a part- or full-time bridge job takes energy and time away from the real job search.

Job seekers must do what they have to in order to meet their needs and those of their family. A bridge job is one approach, but it may not take the pressure off of the job seeker or make finding the real job easier.

Negative Thoughts

Most of us play negative thoughts in our heads. Think back to the last review or feedback you received. You probably received a lot of positive comments on something you did; the negative comments, though, tend to play louder and longer than all of the positive ones.

I refer to this negative soundtrack as the 8-track tape playing in our heads. I use the archaic 8-track tape for my analogy because it is old and was an "endless loop" of tape that would continually play without ever needing to stop. Job seekers are already playing this 8-track tape over and over again with negative comments that someone else said. Then they add in their own soundtrack of doubts and fears.

As the friend, family, or spouse of a job seeker, you need to stop the 8-track tape that is playing in your own head regarding your job seeker's job situation and help your job seeker eject the negative tape playing in their head. (See Illustration 3.3)

You need to process your own feelings about the job seeker's job loss. If you are from the job market of *yesteryear*, you may not be grasping or yet accepting the reality of the new job market. You may still feel that the job loss reflects negatively on your job seeker.

As parents and spouses, you may have part of your own identity wrapped up in the position your loved ones held ("My son's the head of XYZ company", or "I am the wife of the CEO of ZYX Corporation"). The job should not define your loved one nor does the loss of it. In this new job market, we will find our identity in ourselves and our job security will come by keeping our skills and experience in demand.

3.3 – Eject the 8-Track Tape of Negative Thoughts Playing in the Job Seeker's Head

There is no shame in being in a job transition. Once the job seeker has processed their loss, they should let key people know they are looking.

Chapter Summary

Employers do not want to hire anyone who lacks confidence or who has a negative attitude. It is essential that your job seeker give themselves the permission and time to process the loss, do what it takes to choose a positive attitude, and look forward to the opportunities that lie ahead. Your job seeker needs to get help for any pressure points and 211 is a wonderful resource that can help.

Attitude: Additional Reading

The link for updates to *Found a Job Yet?* will provide an updated list of additional books on this topic. RightChanges clients are required to read *Who Moved My Cheese* by Spencer

Johnson and identify which character they are with regard to the job search. Other books to help with Attitude are as follows:

Attitude is Everything – 10 Life Changing Steps to Turning Attitude Into Action by Keith Harrell

The Power of Positive Thinking by Norman Vincent Peale

Believer's Bonus

You may have recognized the source of the plan mentioned above that will prosper your job seeker and not harm them, a plan which will give hope and a future. I refer to this as the job seeker's scripture.

"For I know the plans I have for you", declares the Lord, "plans to prosper you and not to harm you, plans to give you hope and a future. Then you will call upon me and come and pray to me, and I will listen to you. You will seek me and find me when you seek me with all of your heart. I will be found by you", declares the Lord, "and will bring you back from captivity. I

will gather you from all the nations and places where I have

banished you", declares the Lord, "and bring you back to the

place from which I carried you into exile".

– *Jeremiah 29:11-14*

Of course, the Bible is highly suggested reading. When I was in my job search in 2002, someone said reading Psalms and Proverbs was good for anyone in times of trouble. I now suggest it to others as well.

Look for how God may use this time. In 2002, when I was in my job search, God was teaching me to walk in faith. For others, He has used the job transition to give them time with a loved one who was ill or dying. He often uses this time to help people reset their priorities and draw them nearer to Him. We do not always see the reason right away. Continue asking Him and keep looking. He has a plan.

My hope is in you all day long.

– Psalm 25:5

We also rejoice in our sufferings, because we know that suffering produces perseverance; perseverance, character; and character, hope.

– Romans 5:3-4

And we know that in all things God works for the good of those who love him, who have been called according to his purpose.

– Romans 8:28

Being confident of this, that he who began a good work in you will carry it on to completion until the day of Christ Jesus.

– Philippians 1:6

Chapter 4

Aptitude

You Cannot Sell a Product Unless You Know It

Now that the job seeker has processed the loss and accepted that there is opportunity ahead, they need to move on to Step 2 - Aptitude.

Before a salesperson can sell a product, they have to know how the product works and what makes it better than the competition's product. Then they have to frame the features and benefits in a way that demonstrates value to the client. I use a computer as my analogy for this product.

It would be senseless of me to create a brochure for the computer I am selling without understanding the features and competitive advantages. You can also imagine that I would not sell many computers if I walked into the customer's office, and when asked why they should buy *this* computer, I replied, "I don't know", or worse yet, "I need a sale".

The same is true for the job search. Job seekers are selling their skills, experience, and abilities. It is senseless to update the résumé (a piece of the job seeker's marketing materials) without really knowing and being able to articulate their competitive advantage. The job seeker must know how to answer the question "Why should we hire you?"; the answer "I need a job!" will not do.

Job seekers must inventory their abilities, interests, values, education, professional certifications, and technical skills. By inventory, I mean discover them and write them down. They must understand what they liked and disliked about previous jobs, previous managers, and positions in order to make an informed decision about the next company, manager, and position. Because hiring managers use previous performance as an indication of future performance, job seekers need to identify and document their prior accomplishments.

Job seekers learn that there is a particular format to use when relaying their previous accomplishments. This is the STAR format. STAR stands for the Situation or Task that I faced, the Actions I took, and the Results I achieved. By accomplishments I do not mean they cured cancer or solved world peace. Accomplishments are the achievements and contributions the job seeker made; they can include ideas they had, ways they improved processes, or saved the company money.

As a job search coach, I help each of my clients identify and document over 50 STARs, fifty ways they made a difference in their previous jobs.

It is also important for the job seeker to understand what makes them tick. This is a good time to take assessments to understand their personality, strengths, work style, and other things that will help determine what environment is a good fit for them. Organizational fit is an ever increasing trait companies look for and the job seeker needs to understand what a good fit is for them.

Leveraging previous skills is not enough. One of the concerns hiring managers have about candidates who have been out of the workforce for a few months is that they have let their skills atrophy. Job seekers should make use of any downtime during the transition to develop new abilities or enhance existing skills. The job seekers can even use their skills in volunteer capacities.

Online there are an amazing number of free training resources. Search the Internet for the words "free training" and the topic desired. Taking courses not only gives the job seeker a sense of accomplishment but also a great answer when asked by hiring authorities what the job seeker has done since their last job. Not only have they not let their skills atrophy, but they have actually grown new skills making them more marketable. Many companies offer free demos and trial copies of software. Job seekers should make use of these resources to maintain their competitive edge.

Chapter Summary

Job seekers have to know their product before they will be successful in selling it. They need to take the time to identify and document skills, and abilities, take assessments, and enhance and develop new skills.

Aptitude: Additional Reading

StrengthsFinder 2.0 by Tom Rath (includes an online assessment)

What Color is Your Parachute? by Richard Bolles

Believer's Bonus

Encourage your job seeker to discover their God-given gift and purpose. Rick Warren's *Purpose Driven Life* is a good resource.

I praise you because I am fearfully and wonderfully made; your works are wonderful, I know that full well.

– Psalm 139:14

We have different gifts, according to the grace given us. If a man's gift is prophesying, let him use it in proportion to his faith. If it is serving, let him serve; if it is teaching, let him teach; if it is encouraging, let him encourage; if it is contributing to the needs of others, let him give generously; if it is leadership, let him govern diligently; if it is showing mercy, let him do it cheerfully.

– Romans 12:6-8

Each one should use whatever gift he has received to serve others.

– 1 Peter 4:10

Chapter 5

Altitude

Where to Work and Who is Hiring

Altitude is another term for determining who is hiring and where the job seeker wants to work.

Continuing with the analogy of selling a computer, I would not be successful if I tried to sell my computer at a neighborhood pharmacy. It can be a great pharmacy, but no one goes there to buy a computer. If they saw the computer for sale there, they would think it could not be very good, even at a low price, because it is being sold in a pharmacy.

I also would not want to develop the brochure for the computer until I know what market I am targeting. Is this computer the one college graduates want? Is it for users who are looking for high-end graphics? Is this computer suited for businesses that need a durable computer that can be taken into the field and abused?

In the same way, job seekers must identify their requirements: the position, industry, location, and salary. Job seekers must also identify who is hiring and which companies they want to target.

Cast a Wider Net?

Some people have the misconception that they should cast a wider net and be more general in what they are looking for. The opposite is true. Say you are drilling for water. If you spend your time drilling a lot of holes, it takes longer to reach the water table than if you concentrate on drilling a few holes deeply. (Illustration 5.1) A more targeted approach is more successful.

5.1 – A Targeted Approach is Best

Only when job seekers know their competitive

advantages and who they are targeting (the companies) can they

develop successful marketing materials.

Exploring Options

When a person loses a job, it is an opportunity to assess

what they really want to do with their life. Many job seekers

have successfully pursued careers outside of the one they have

held previously. Personally, I had over twenty years in

Information Technology and am now a successful job search coach, public speaker, author of this book, and have written articles that are read worldwide. Being a job search coach is not a normal career path for most people in IT; I refer to it as a left turn.

The job transition may be a good time for the job seeker to reinvent themselves and pursue their passions. It is never too late. If they do not know what it is they want to do, a career coach can help the job seeker identify career options.

The job seeker should be careful in choosing a career coach who does not exclude options because of their own biases. I had a client who started working with me after seeing another career coach. In reviewing the other career coach's report, I saw a comment that one option the job seeker might consider was not a viable option. I found out it was not the client's opinion but that of the career coach. True, there are jobs where people do not make a lot of money or where they make a lot of money but very few people get to that level. In my opinion though, if there are people doing that work and getting paid and it is the job seeker's passion, it should be explored. Let the facts rule it out, not fear or biases.

The job seeker can conduct informational interviews with people who are already working in the field they are exploring. The job seeker can ask how the person got into the job, the good aspects of the job, as well as the bad and ugly aspects of the work. Someone in that field can also share what other positions exist in that field and advise what, if any, additional skills or experience are needed. These are the facts that should eliminate a position, not a person's bias or fear.

Other job seekers have tapped into the passion they had earlier in life, the one they had before they took the career that others thought they should have, and are successfully pursuing those passions.

Purchasing a franchise or starting their own business are other choices job seekers are successful at pursuing.

In numerous recent articles , passion was determined to be a distinguishing factor between candidates. [5-1] Even if a job seeker does not end up changing industries or careers, this is a great time to confirm they are on the right track with their lives.

Chapter Summary

Before the job seeker can create or update their résumé and other marketing materials and begin the job search, they have to know where they want to work and who is hiring. In determining what work they want to do and where they want to work, the job seeker should consider tapping into their passions.

Altitude: Additional Reading

In most major cities there is a business paper and many are a part of The Biz Journal brand. Go to www.bizjournal.com to get the name of the business journal for your area. For Atlanta the Biz Journal is the Atlanta Business Chronicle. For Chicago there is Crain's Chicago Business.

Book of Lists is published by the regional biz journals and is a

resource to identify target companies.

Believer's Bonus

"For I know the plans I have for you", declares the Lord, "plans

to prosper you and not to harm you, plans to give you hope and

a future".

– Jeremiah 29:11

Show me your ways, O Lord, teach me your paths; guide me in

your truth and teach me for you are God my Savior.

– Psalm 25:4-5

"I am the Lord your God, who teaches you what is the best for

you, who directs you in the way you should go."

– Isaiah 48:17

Stand at the crossroads and look; ask for the ancient paths, ask where the good way is, and walk in it and you will find rest for your souls.

– Jeremiah 6:16

For we are God's workmanship, created in Christ Jesus to do works, which God prepared in advance for us to do.

– Ephesians 2:10

Chapter 6

Marketing Materials

It is Much More Than a Résumé

The job seeker has chosen a good attitude, inventoried skills, abilities, and accomplishments and has identified their target careers and target companies. In the next chapter, we will continue with Step 4. Now is the right time for the job seeker to update their marketing materials.

In today's job market, there are many more pieces to a job seeker's marketing collateral than just a résumé.

The following is the *minimum* inventory of marketing materials needed for today's job seeker.

This book will not get into the detail needed by the job seeker about each item of marketing material. It is an introduction for you so, as a member of the job seeker's support team, you know what is now required.

It is essential that each article of the job seeker's marketing collateral give a consistent message and have the same look and feel.

Résumé

The résumé is, was, and will be a document that describes a job seeker's career that is relevant to the current job search. In prior years, the résumé was more reflective while in more recent years, it has become more "targeted".

Résumé formats and the handling of résumés have changed over the years. Today, there are hundreds if not thousands of résumés submitted for some positions. Résumés sometimes go through a software program that searches for particular terms, or keywords, set up by the hiring authorities.

As few as 10% of the résumés have the keywords needed to make it through the software program, leaving a stack that still contains hundreds of résumés. [6-1] The hiring manager will take a batch of résumés from the resulting stack to review; the others may never get reviewed. The hiring authority may only give each résumé an 8 – 12 second glance.

Many of the old practices used in writing a résumé are no longer in vogue (for example, adding the phrase "References Available Upon Request" is old school).

There are newer formats that provide the job seeker the biggest advantage. The best formats put the selling points in the top half of the first page, or what is called "above the fold", to make the biggest impact in the few seconds the résumé is reviewed.

Chronological job history is not the most important part of the résumé anymore. The common wisdom is that previous accomplishments are an indication of future performance. Therefore, the job seeker needs to leverage the accomplishments they documented during the Aptitude phase to power up the résumé.

These are just a few of the changes to résumés over the past few years.

Cover Letter

The purpose of the cover letter is to establish rapport with the reader and encourage them to give serious consideration to the résumé.

Most hiring managers say they only read the cover letter if they know it has been customized for the position. [6-2] The normal paragraph-formatted cover letters are not read by hiring managers or recruiters.

I recommend the "T" cover letter format. The "T" cover letter format visually walks the reader through why the writer is the perfect candidate. A link to my article about the "T" cover letter is provided at the end of this chapter.

Networking Cards

In the world of business, the most acceptable method for exchanging contact information is the business card, and that holds true during a job transition as well. Business cards or networking cards are not very expensive; some online sites offer them for free, other than the price of shipping. Job seekers should have their networking cards on them at all times.

Elevator Pitch

6.1 The Elevator Pitch

The Elevator Pitch is the 30-second response the job seeker should give when asked the question "What do you do?"

It contains the following core elements:

- The job seekers name

- Job title and level (senior manager, director of finance, entry level data entry, etc.)

- Industry

- What makes them unique (their brand; more on branding later in this chapter)

- Location (For example: metro Atlanta area, willing to relocate within the Southeast)

- Closing question, in the form of a question, asking the listener who they know in that industry

The elevator pitch is not historical. It should never contain the phrase "I used to…" It should instead communicate what the job seeker is looking for.

List of Accomplishments in STAR Format

The list of accomplishments is developed in the Aptitude step and some of the accomplishments will be used to power up the résumé. The accomplishment list will also be used in the Interview step (Step 5) to add detailed examples to make the answers more real. The accomplishment list is also helpful for job seekers to re-read when they start to feel down about themselves so they remember how talented and accomplished they are.

LinkedIn Profile

The job search has now ventured into the world of social networking. LinkedIn is the most leveraged social network for connecting with other people for business purposes, including the job search. Although some job search activity is moving to Facebook and Twitter, having a profile and being active on LinkedIn is required. This includes a professional photograph and posting at least three recommendations from their contacts.

If these are new concepts to you, you may want to read one of the books I recommend about LinkedIn at the end of this chapter.

Reference List

References, both personal and professional, are still checked by hiring authorities to support the information given by the job seeker.

Although the reference list is only to be given out when a company requests it, usually when they have passed the initial screening, the job seeker should take time to identify their references and confirm the latest contact information for each reference.

Brand Statement

The job market is taking many tips and best practices from the world of marketing. One such practice is the use of a brand statement. The brand statement and tag line can be used on networking cards and other marketing materials to help keep the job seeker in the mind of the reader. It summarizes how the job seeker is unique and how the company will benefit from it.

The tag line for RightChanges is "The Affordable and Successful Job Search Coach".

Target Companies

Up to this point, I have been referring to companies as the future employer. By "companies" I include corporations, franchises, non-profit organizations, governmental agencies, and even self-owned businesses.

An unfocused approach to the job search has proven to be less successful; it waters down the job search effort. Job seekers need to identify the job they are pursuing and 10 – 15 companies they want to work for so they can focus their networking efforts. Note: most jobs are available in smaller companies. [6-3]

Networking Guide

You want to help the job seeker in the search. Job seekers need to give people in their network (which includes you) something specific to do to help them. Handing you a résumé

may not be helpful for you (unless you are a recruiter or hiring

manager) because it says what the person did, not what they are

looking for.

The Networking Guide is a one page document that

gives key words to listen for in everyday encounters. When you

meet someone who is hiring one of the titles listed or works at

one of the target companies, an introduction to the job seeker is

in order. There will be more on this in the chapters regarding

what you should do to help.

Chapter Summary

As you can see with just the marketing materials

required, the job search is a lot more complicated than ever

before.

The job seeker needs to develop a set of marketing

materials that have a consistent look and feel and consistently communicate the job seeker's value and consistently show how the company will benefit by hiring them.

Marketing Materials: Additional Reading

Cover Letter: *The Most Powerful Cover Letter* by Judi Adams at RightChangesJobSearchCoach.blogspot.com

Networking Guide: *What Document is as Valuable to a Job Seeker as a Great Résumé* by Judi Adams at RightChangesJobSearchCoach.blogspot.com

Knock'em Dead Cover Letters by Martin Yate

Believer's Bonus

> *The integrity of the upright guides them, but the unfaithful are destroyed by their duplicity.*
>
> *– Proverbs 11:3*

"You shall not give false testimony against your neighbor"

– Exodus 20:16

From the fruit of his lips a man is filled with good things as

surely as the work of his hands rewards him.

– Proverbs 12:14

Do you see a man skilled in his work? He will serve before

kings; he will not serve before obscure men.

– Proverbs 22:29

Chapter 7

Search

The Approaches to Finding a Job

Now that the job seeker has developed a set of marketing materials, they can search for the job. There are a number of tactics that a job seeker can employ to find the job opportunities.

Using the wrong approach to finding a job is like driving a horse and buggy on the interstate. (Illustration 7.1) The driver may get there, but it will take a lot longer and may not be the most enjoyable ride.

7.1 - The Wrong Job Search Approach is Like Driving a Horse and Buggy on the

Interstate

The following details the various approaches and the success rate associated with each.

Job Fairs

Television news broadcasts, newspapers, and other media sources frequently announce job fairs that are being held in town. Each job fair is sponsored by a company, governmental agency, or job fair organizer. There is usually no charge to job seekers for attending these events. There may be, though, a participation fee charged to the employers for hosting booths or tables. These fees are used to help offset the costs associated with sponsoring the fair.

Many jobs seekers know firsthand that at such events, the companies' representatives do not have time to speak to each and every candidate that approaches the booth. It is not unusual for the representatives to do nothing more than take a copy of the candidate's résumé, add it to a pile of other résumés, and tell the job seeker to apply online. Attending job fairs just to be told to apply online can be very demoralizing.

In today's job market, there are many more people looking for jobs than there are jobs available, so there is no shortage of résumés coming into companies from other sources. It usually is not necessary, or the best use of employers' money and their employees' time, to host booths at job fairs. The biggest benefit to the company is the goodwill the company generates by taking part in such events.

If not corporations, then who participates in job fairs? Many job fairs are staffed by colleges and universities, technical schools, and outplacement firms, not with the goal of hiring people but to sell their services. The different branches of the military may be represented as well with the goal of recruiting. In addition, government agencies may participate to attract candidates that otherwise would not have considered a government job. A job seeker just does not have to stand in line and wade through crowds of people to consider those options. Their time might be better spent using other approaches.

When using this approach though, the job seeker can make the most of job fairs by contacting the fair sponsor ahead of time and requesting a list of participating companies. It is usually possible to also get the total number and types of jobs these employers are offering.

The success rate of getting a job by attending a job fair is very low since candidates have very little time with company representatives and are directed to apply online which they could have done without attending.

School Career Fairs

A corporate recruiter once told me that her company hires more frequently from school and university career fairs then normal job fairs because recent graduates have training on the latest technologies and techniques. Although recent graduates do not have a lot of job experience, they also do not cost as much as job seekers with years of experience.

Even if they are not a recent graduate, the job seeker can still contact their school to get information about upcoming career fairs and, unless otherwise specified, can attend. They should still request a list of participating companies and the number and types of jobs these companies are offering to be sure it is worthwhile.

School career fairs yield a bit more success than regular job fairs yet, since these are only scheduled periodically, the job seeker does not want to rely solely on that approach for finding a job.

Newspaper Ads

The help wanted ads section in local newspapers used to be the number one place to look for job leads. Watch any old TV show or movie and you will see a job seeker circling ads in the paper. Those days are over. Companies are using other methods (for example, online job boards such as CareerBuilder) to get the word out. What used to be page after page of "Help Wanted" ads now in some papers barely takes up two columns.

Internet Job Boards

Some of the positions that used to be posted in the newspaper are now posted on the commercial online job boards (Monster, CareerBuilder, etc.) or the specific company's web site. Listing aggregators such as Indeed.com scan other job sites and compile a comprehensive list of open positions.

For some posted positions, hundreds if not thousands of résumés are received in just a matter of days yet sometimes as few as 10% of the candidates are qualified. Why would a job seeker apply for a position they are not qualified for? Some job seekers are under the misguided concept that Human Resources (HR) or the hiring manager will look at all of the résumés and take the time to find another position for them within the company.

Social Networking and Social Media

With the advent and adoption of social networking (Facebook, LinkedIn, etc.) and social media sites, jobs are now being found through, and success tracked for, these sources. The success rate is around 2-6%.[7-1]

The Hidden Job Market

Recent estimates are that only an approximate 15% of all of the available jobs are publicized. Instead companies are choosing to use other methods to get the word out about positions. The 75-95% of positions not posted are referred to as the "hidden" job market. [7-2]

Many companies do not post positions because they prefer to have employees' referrals. These candidates are usually former coworkers of the employees and therefore more likely qualified for the position.

In some cases, a position is not posted because there is a person serving in that role already who is about to be let go for performance reasons and, if the position is posted, the existing employee may see it, tipping off the company's plan.

Another reason a position may not be posted is that, although the company knows what skills they need, they are not ready to start the laborious process of receiving résumés and fielding phone calls.

There are a number of other reasons positions are not publicized but, whatever the reason, not all open positions will not be found in the paper or on the Internet.

Keyword Software

Many companies are utilizing application management systems and software that scan résumés for certain keywords. If a résumé does not have the acceptable percentage of keywords, the résumé is rejected. Of the remaining tens and hundreds of qualified résumés, only a small percentage of them will be scanned by a human. Picture it: the person responsible for selecting candidates for an interview faces a pile of 100 résumés. They may take a selection of résumés from the top or middle of the pile to review. It can be pure chance that a résumé is selected for review even if it passed the keyword search software.

The statistic quoted on the number of job seekers who get their job applying online is approximately 25%. That 25% is going after only 15% of the available jobs. Those are not great odds. [7-1]

Unless the job seeker is one of the candidates selected, they rarely hear back on the applications they submit online, creating a deeper sense of isolation and failure for the job seeker.

Recruiters

Some companies pay recruiting firms to help identify qualified candidates. Since the company pays for this service, there is no charge to the job seeker.

Note: There are some recruiting firms that charge a fee, usually a substantial one, to job seekers and say they guarantee they will find them a job. No firm can guarantee the person will get a job unless the recruiting firm hires them since those are the only jobs they control. The guarantee usually means a portion of the fee is refundable if the candidate does not find a job. Many consumer advocates and job search experts suggest staying clear of any recruiter that charges the candidate.

Before the advent of keyword search software, companies leveraged recruiters to help weed through the flood of résumés to find the best candidates for the job. Recruiters then presented a number of candidates that meet the requirements. Recruiters may not care which of the candidates are eventually hired; they just want one of the candidates they represent to get hired so the company gets paid. They want a happy client, who is the company, not the job seeker. When a job seeker uses a recruiter as the primary job search strategy, they are putting the job search in the hands of someone whose primary interest is not that of the candidate, but instead the company.

The statistic quoted on the number of job seekers who get their job by working with recruiters is an estimated 11% and the recruiter may not care if it is your job seeker or another candidate they represent who gets the job. [7-1] According to a recruiter friend of mine, job seekers should put very kittle reliance on recruiters for landing that next job.

Networking

Networking is not a new approach to finding a job. In fact, networking has been around since the start of civilization.

In previous years, people automatically networked because they lived in smaller towns where everyone knew everyone else.

Since the world has become a more mobile society, where we might not even know our next door neighbor, networking has to be an intentional activity.

Networking is not complicated. It merely means having a friend or contact that knows the job seeker and introducing them to someone who knows someone who is looking for a person with their skills or qualities. Whether it is a family member, a friend of a friend, or a new contact, many jobs were and are found going through someone who knows someone. It is about both who you know and who knows you.

The statistic quoted on the number of job seekers who get their jobs through networking is greater than 45% and it is through networking that you can find the hidden job market. [7-1]

For many people, networking is out of their comfort zone. They do not like doing it, and they do not think they are good at it. Like anything new, the job seeker needs to learn how to do it, practice it, and then do it. Will it ever be something they love to do? Maybe not. But it is something that is required for the rest of their lives.

An Overall Approach

Job seekers are successful finding jobs using each of these approaches. Knowing the success rates for each will help job seekers know where to spend the bulk of their time.

Are we suggesting that job seekers not go to job or school career fairs, not apply to ads, and not use recruiters? Not at all. What is recommended is that job seekers spend a proportional amount of time using a particular approach based on its success rate. Therefore the majority of a job seeker's time should be spent on networking and no more than 25% of their time applying to online ads. Even for the jobs they apply to online, the job seeker still needs to network into the company to increase their chances of being interviewed.

Too many job seekers (in my estimation up to 80%) limit themselves to applying online and months or years later are still baffled that they have not found a job. Is it the easiest way to apply for a job? Certainly! It is just not the most effective approach and could greatly lengthen the time it takes to find a job.

Each networking event may bring the job seeker closer to their desired job. Measuring the progress of the job search by the number of applications submitted is ill-conceived.

Where to Network

As we have seen, networking is a very successful and the most underutilized approach to finding job opportunities. Developing and leveraging contacts is the key.

Level 1 contacts are those that the job seeker knows well. This includes family, friends, former coworkers, etc.

Level 2 contacts are those that the job seeker's Level 1 contacts know or ones who are close acquaintances of the job seeker. These include friends and contacts of parents, of the spouse, and friends of friends, as well as the job seeker's doctor, dentist, hair stylist/barber, or people from clubs, associations, and activities in which the job seeker is involved.

Job seekers may leverage their Level 1 and 2 contacts and not get a qualified lead. For this reason, it is beneficial for the job seeker to increase their network.

There are a number of ways to develop new contacts.

Job Networking Groups

In many cities, there are numerous job networking groups. Many are church based; others are not. Crossroads Career Network is one nationwide job networking group. I am affiliated with Crossroads and led the chapter at my church.

In addition to developing new contacts, the benefits of job networking groups include the following:

- Learning new job search tips
- Sharing experiences with other job seekers
- Receiving encouragement during the job search

Job seekers should not limit themselves to job networking groups, though, because most of the people in attendance are also in a job transition. Although they usually have information about companies that are hiring, they are not the hiring managers.

See Appendix D about starting a Crossroads in your community.

Industry Networking Groups

Networking groups, whether based on job skills (PMI for Project Manager, IIBA for Business Analyst for instance) or based on industry (SHRM for HR) are target-rich environments for networking. Most of the people in attendance are employed and include hiring managers or employees. These employed participants may be looking for people to refer for one of the hidden jobs in their company. These groups can be found using the job seeker's favorite search engine and typing in the name of the industry or career and the word "network", or "networking", or "association" (without the quote marks), example: business analyst association. Industry networking groups are an excellent place for the job seeker to network.

Groups with Common Interests

Groups where people share common interests are also great places to network. For example, even if the job seeker is looking for a job in IT, if they are interested in photography, the job seeker should consider networking at a photography networking group. The common interest serves as a foundation on which to build trust and when there is trust, people will make their network available.

Other Contacts

Every daily interaction is an opportunity to develop a new contact. It just requires the job seeker to get out of the house and interact with other people.

Volunteerism is a great way to establish contacts while helping others. It may also be an opportunity to hone existing skills or develop new ones.

By adding in small non-job-search related activities, such as working out in a neighborhood fitness center, the job seeker can increase their sense of accomplishment and self-esteem and possibly expand their network.

As a result of being unemployed, job seekers feel disconnected from life because they are no longer going to work every day and interacting with other people. Job seekers need to make a calendar of events to attend in the coming weeks and months. The calendar of events provides them a goal to reach and, when completed, they will have a sense of accomplishment as they mark things as done. Getting out of the house and among other people also helps the job seeker feel connected and not as alone.

Chapter Summary

We examined the various approaches your loved one has at their disposal to find the job opportunities and the success rates associated with each.

Creating and maintaining a calendar of planned activities and meetings will add back the structure and sense of purpose that was lost with the job. Being intentional about the job search helps your job seeker make the most of each day.

Search: Additional Reading

How to Get Your Point Across in 30 Seconds or Less

by Milo O. Frank

How to Work a Room – Your Essential Guide to Savvy Socializing by

Susan RoAne

Face To Face by Susan RoAne

The Art of Mingling by Jeanne Martinet

Dig Your Well Before You're Thirsty by Harvey Mackay

The Definitive Book of Body Language by Allan and Barbara Pease

Believer's Bonus

> *But I trust in you, O Lord; I say "You are my God". My times*
> *are in your hands.*
>
> *– Psalm 31:14*

Trust in the Lord with all your heart and lean not on your own understanding; in all your ways acknowledge him, and he will make your paths straight.

– Proverbs 3: 5-6

Commit to the Lord whatever you do, and your plans will succeed.

– Proverbs 16:3

In his heart a man plans his course, but the Lord determines his steps.

– Proverbs 16:9

"Seek first his kingdom and his righteousness, and all these things will be given to you as well."

– Matthew 6:33

Chapter 8

Sort

The Interview

Securing the interview is the goal of every job seeker because it is the step before the job offer. There is so much riding on a successful interview.

Think about it though. When nothing except bragging rights are on the line, there are not many people who would enter a neighborhood championship (be it tennis, golf, badminton, or horseshoes) without practicing or warming up. Yet when a job is on the line, too many job seekers go into interviews without practicing. Job seekers need to know how to prepare for and practice interviewing.

There are 4 Ps of a successful interview. Job seekers first need to understand the purpose of the interview (there are actually two purposes: the company's purpose and the interviewee's purpose for the interview), the preparation that must be done, how to successfully handle the interview (performance) and the steps following the interview (post interview).

Some job networking groups sponsor mock interviews where job seekers are interviewed by skilled hiring managers or recruiters. Since a real job is not on the line, the interviewer can provide honest feedback about what the job seeker did well in the interview and areas they will want to improve.

Many job search coaches, including yours truly, offer customized, filmed mock interview services.

In a later chapter, there will be ideas on how you can help with this step.

Chapter Summary

The interview is so important. The job seeker should not go into it without preparing, practicing, and follow-up with the hiring authority.

Sort: Additional Reading

101 Dynamite Questions to Ask at Your Job Interview by Richard Fein

Interview Magic by Susan Britton Whitcomb

Believer's Bonus

Before and after the interview, you and the job seeker should pray for open doors if the job is God's will (the plan He has) and closed doors if it is not. The toughest part is praising God when doors close. It is the answer to your prayer though, and He should be praised for answering it.

Delight yourself in the Lord and he will give you the desires of your heart.

– Psalm 37:4

Be still before the Lord and wait patiently for him…

– Psalm 37:7

Trust in the Lord will all of your heart and lean not on your own understanding…

– Proverbs 3:5

In his heart a man plans his course, but the Lord determines his steps.

– Proverbs 16:9

This is what the Lords says – your Redeemer, the Holy One of Israel: "I am the Lord your God, who teaches you what is best for you, who directs you in the way you should go."

– Isaiah 48:17

The Lord will guide you always; he will satisfy your needs in a sun-scorched land and will strengthen your frame.

– Isaiah 58:11

Chapter 9

Select

Choosing the Right Job

An offer is in hand. The job seeker has worked hard to get to this place. When a job seeker is offered a position, they need to understand the opportunity and compare it to the requirements they identified during the Altitude (Step 1). They should accept the job only if it is right for them.

If there are questions about the position, benefits, or expectations, these should be clarified before taking the position.

The job seeker should not necessarily jump at the first opportunity that comes along. During Steps 2 and 3 (Aptitude and Altitude), the job seeker defined what they want and need, what the right position and company looks like for them, and where they will thrive. These should be factored into the decision.

There is more harm in taking the wrong job than having no job at all. [9-1] Many of us have been in jobs or working for companies where we were miserable. We do not wish a miserable job on others, especially your job seeker. Job seekers should have a peace about the job they are considering before they take it. Taking a job just because it is the first one to come along can set the job seeker up for a job or company where they may be unhappy or where they will not succeed. A failure could send the person and job search back to Step 1 – Attitude, and this setback will be hard to explain in the next interview.

Now is the time to potentially negotiate. The job seeker should conduct salary research on websites such as salary.com and indeed.com to determine current salary based on experience and locale. Even in this economy, people have been successful at negotiating a higher salary and more vacation time.

Remember, this is a new job market. The rules have changed. It is okay to take a job and leave it when something better comes along if the person does so professionally.

Chapter Summary

The offer has been received. The job seeker should make the best decision based on the criteria they previously established.

Believer's Bonus

Delight yourself in the Lord and he will give you the desires of your heart. Commit your way to the Lord; trust in him and he will do this: He will make your righteousness shine like the dawn, the justice of your cause like the noonday sun. Be still before the Lord and wait patiently for him.

– Psalm 37:4-7

If the Lord delights in a man's way, he makes his steps firm; though he stumble, he will not fall, for the Lord upholds him with his hand.

– Psalm 37:23-24

"I am the Lord your God, who teaches you what is the best for you, who directs you in the way you should go."

– Isaiah 48:17

The Lord will guide you always; he will satisfy your needs in a sun-scorched land and will strengthen your frame.

– Isaiah 58:11

Chapter 10

Action Items Once Wonderfully Employed

Congratulations! Your job seeker is now employed in a job they wanted. Remember, though, the reality of today's job market is that your job seeker's next job probably will not be their last. Most of us will be in a job transition again.

Before we review the actions the new employee needs to take to be ready for the next job transition, we will examine the transition they are now facing - one from being a job seeker to being employed again.

The Transition to the New Job

We need to understand the impact of the new job, especially emotionally.

When your job seeker lands the new job, there are more changes the job seeker and the family go through.

The job seeker is now facing a new routine and starts to feel the doubts almost everyone feels when starting a new job. The new employee may fear failing in the new position. There are so many unknowns, and they must learn things that come with getting a new job including the new commute, company, building, people, and routine.

This fear and uncertainty dissipates with time. Reminding the job seeker how they felt this fear before when starting a new job, and yet succeeded in that role, will reassure the job seeker how these feelings are natural and temporary.

Action Items for Life

Now that the employee has started the new job, there are actions they need to take while employed to make the next job transition easier. This list applies to all employed people, so I will write this list directed to you.

- Maintain contacts. Do not wait until you need something to get in touch with people in your network.

- Develop new contacts, within your department, other departments in the company, and within the industry.

- Maintain your marketing materials including your LinkedIn profile, accomplishment list, and inventories of education and technical skills. In addition to having the accomplishment list available should the job end, you can also give it to your manager before they have written your performance review. Downplay it by saying "This is something I do for myself. If you can use it for the performance review, great. If not, that is okay because I am maintaining it for me anyway". Smart managers will not only appreciate it; they may even ask their other direct reports to do the same thing.

[Side note to managers: Consider asking your team members to start maintaining their list of accomplishments, growing list of skills, and education. They should do this for themselves and it will make your life easier at review time. Have your team forward to you copies of kudos that they receive about their work and pass this along to your management. Management gets a lot of bad news; be the source of good news. Showing your management how well your team is doing in the eyes of others reflects positively on you.]

- Maintain your marketable skills. If the company offers training, take it. If the company does not offer training, take it anyway; invest in yourself and your future by paying for it yourself. Before you take classes just for fun, make sure you have taken training that increases your marketability.

- Jim Collins, author of the fabulous book *Good to Great*, was speaking at an event in 2008 and, in response to the question "What is the one word of advice you would give recent graduates?" said, "Do not spend five years getting two years of experience". [10-1]

It took me weeks, if not months, to process this wisdom. This was contrary to the way I was raised. We used to call people who changed jobs every few years "job hoppers" and it was not a term of affection. Instead, in today's job market people who work for a company for a decade or two are now at a huge disadvantage. They are thought not to have the broad experience that those who have worked for multiple companies in numerous roles have.

Look at companies who groom executives. They usually move the candidate around to different departments to get a broad range of experience. Do the same for yourself.

- Consumer advocates and financial advisors highly recommend that everyone save between 8 and 12 months of salary in ready cash for the next transition.

- Pay it forward. Assist others. There will be people in your transition who would not give you the time of day and others who went out of their way to help you out. How do you want to be perceived?

Chapter Summary

The process is not over once the job seeker is employed. There are actions all of us need to take to be ready for the next transition.

Believer's Bonus

May he give you the desires of your heart and make all your

plans succeed. We will shout for joy when you are

victorious...May the Lord grant you all your requests.

– Psalm 20: 4–5

You have granted him the desire of his heart and have not

withheld the request of his lips.

– Psalm 21:2

For we are God's workmanship, created in Christ Jesus to do

works, which God prepared in advance for us to do.

– Ephesians 2:10

Chapter 11

Additional Challenges

There are groups of people who have additional challenges in finding a job in today's market. As a friend, family member, or spouse of a job seeker, you just need to be aware of these additional challenges.

The Recent Graduate

The challenge for recent graduates is that they have very little work experience and are competing for jobs against people with years of experience. There are, however, advantages that recent graduates have to offer over experienced workers that they need to understand and leverage.

Young people are entering a very mixed generational job market and work force. They need to be aware of and handle the differences that exist between generations.

Interpersonal skills are areas recent graduates need to master. Active listening is one such skill which includes unplugging from technology completely when involved in any conversation, especially and not limited to networking or interviewing. The ability to read body language is another skill a recent graduate would be well advised to learn.

Appearance plays a key role in the job search, so young people need to understand that the apparel that was acceptable in school may not be acceptable in the job search. A work-appropriate wardrobe is a worthwhile expense.

Proving their work ethic, when they may not have held a full time job before, is crucial. Highlighting part time work and internships is important.

At the top of hiring manager's list of concerns for recent graduates are their writing skills. I have seen this for myself. In business e-mail messages and thank you notes from students, I have seen the use of text message lingo and improper grammar.

These are just a few of the extra challenges young people who are just entering the workforce face.

The Experienced Worker

People with a lot of experience are being rejected with the term "overqualified". This term is used to disguise other unspoken concerns. Experienced workers need to understand the hidden messages and proactively address them in all aspects of the job search (marketing materials, skills, personal appearance, and during the interview).

Speaking of personal appearance, there may be expenses associated with the de-aging process if the person has not kept their appearance contemporary. New contemporary eye glasses, a more up-to-date wardrobe and fashionable accessories may be required. This will be a worthwhile investment.

People Re-entering the Workforce

Whether coming out of retirement or re-joining the work force after taking time to raise a family, people re-entering the workforce have the challenge of competing with other seekers who have more recent work experience. People re-entering the work force need to demonstrate they have not let their skills atrophy by sharing the transferable skills they have continued to use and new skills gained since leaving the workforce.

Chapter Summary

The job market is tough as it is, and there are additional challenges certain groups of people will encounter. These challenges can be overcome; the job seeker just needs to be aware of them and the techniques required to handle these challenges.

Believer's Bonus

Gray hair is a crown of splendor; it is attained by a righteous
life.

– Proverbs 16:31

Do not rebuke an older man harshly, but exhort him as if he
were your father. Treat younger men as brothers, older women
as mothers, and younger women as sisters, with absolute
purity.

– 1 Timothy 5:1-2

Part II

Develop a Plan

to be Supportive

Chapter 12

Understand What the Job Seeker Considers as

Supportive

Now that you have an understanding of the new job market and what it requires, let us examine various ways you can be supportive and helpful to your job seeker. We will also cover some pitfalls that well intentioned supporters fall into that actually hurt more than help.

You have heard the expression, "It is the thought that counts." So we need to put thought into it.

It is important to understand what your job seeker considers supportive. Even though the golden rule is "do unto others as you would have them do unto you", people want, need, and value different things. See Illustration 12.1.

As a senior manager in Information Technology, I learned that the people working for me are all individuals and I could not use the same approach to motivate them all. Some team members wanted recognition, and others would rather die than get public recognition. The same is true of all people. Each person has something that makes them feel appreciated and supported.

12.1 – A Gift May Have More Value to One Person than Another

A fabulous book on this topic is Gary Chapman and Paul White's *The Five Languages of Appreciation in the Workplace*. One of the basic principles of the book is that "appreciation needs to be viewed as valuable to the recipient in order to have an impact". There are five languages defined in Chapman and White's book.

If you have not read this book, I highly recommend you do. The principles outlined are helpful in all relationships, business or otherwise.

If your job seeker's language of appreciation is not service, your offer to help them with the job search does not mean as much to them. You should determine what you can do to help them feel appreciated.

Ask your job seeker to help you help them. Ask them to read *The Five Languages of Appreciation in the Workplace* and let you know their languages of appreciation. If they are willing to read it, you may want to offer to buy the book for them or loan them your copy. By knowing their own language of appreciation the job seeker will be better equipped to determine what job is a fit for them.

Parents: Gary Chapman has published a book titled *How to Really Love Your Adult Child* and it takes you beyond the advice where other books stop (the teenage years) and shares how to continue parenting once they are young adults.

Spouses: There is a version of this book for married couples titled *The Five Love Languages*. You have your own "love language" too and the job search affects you directly. Each of you should read *The Five Love Languages* to identify your love languages and then review the results together.

Chapter Summary

Ask your job seeker to read *The Five Languages* of *Appreciation in the Workplace* and once you understand what your job seeker considers as supportive, be sure to tailor your support and encouragement of them in a way they appreciate.

Believer's Bonus

"Do to others as you would have them do to you."

– Luke 6:31

Chapter 13

Understand What Job Seekers are Feeling

Many job seekers shared that the people closest to them accused them of not really trying to find a job or implied that somehow being unemployed was their fault.

By reading the previous chapters, you have seen how the job market has changed, and it is not the fault of the individual that it is harder, and usually takes longer, to find a job. You now understand that a job seeker will be in a job transition more times than ever before in history. You now have a better understanding of what it takes for today's job seeker to find a job.

Your job seeker is not in a job transition because they want to be. Acknowledge to them that you now have a better understanding of the new job market. Ask them how they are feeling and listen. It will mean so much to them. There will be more on the active practice of listening in Chapter 15.

According to the research conducted by the Pew Research Center of the job seekers during the great recession 39-46% report strain in family relationships. Results from the research showed that 29-38% of job seekers reported loss of some self-respect. [13-1]

In the Voice of Job Seekers

Here is what the job seekers said they are going through and feeling:

> *[You] become uncertain of your place in the work force. Depression creeps in to some degree and your value declines in your own mind.*
>
> *– Phillip D.*

In this job search, most of the hiring managers or job boards never actually talk to me, get to know me or my personality. It makes me feel like a non-person sometimes. The worst thing for me is when there is no response at all. No phone calls, no e-mails. Just indifference. Another thing I have noticed ... people with jobs have a real disconnect from those of us who have been searching for work.
- Monselle V.

The worst thing that people did was not acknowledge that I was going through a big change in my life...after working 28 years for the same organization!!!
– Liz H.

I think the worst thing a friend or former colleague can say to you is wondering why you are out of work for so long when you know you have [been] diligent[ly] busting your butt every day and evening turning over every rock to find your next career. The expression of "if you only knew" is hard for them to comprehend when they have not walked in your shoes!!

– Al F.

Worst [thing a person did]: ignored how difficult an extended search can be during these times and instead told me what he or she would do to search (very antiquated advice, I might add).

– Patty F.

I was basically on my own during the search. I got so many conflicting pieces of advice and job leads that it was up to me to figure which path to take.

– Bernadette E.

There are too many people acting as if "it's not their problem" that we have so many people unemployed. What they don't seem to realize is, they just might be standing in the unemployment [line] next. The person you help today

could be the one that helps you tomorrow.

  – Judy C.

I have been looking for a job coming up on a year now, and I

never thought it would take me so long.

  – Ilene L.

Chapter Summary

Understand and acknowledge what your job seeker is feeling about being in this transition.

Chapter 14

Be There and Stay in Touch

As you read the feedback received from the poll of job seekers, the most consistent theme was the isolation they feel. Part of this is real; the job seeker no longer has structure to their day. There is no formal place to go every weekday where there are people to interact with, no clear purpose, and no sense of accomplishment at the end of each day. It is also true that some people withdraw from the job seeker during this time either because the person does not know what to say or is uncomfortable being around someone who is going through a tough time.

The sense of withdrawal by others happens with people who have gone through any type of loss (death, divorce, bankruptcy, etc.). People who do not know what to say pull away out of their own discomfort. There are some people who pull away out of some odd sense that bad luck rubs off.

Some of the feelings of isolation, though, are imagined by the job seeker as a result of the increased need for interaction. You may not have withdrawn, but you may not have stepped up to fill the void they are experiencing. It may feel to them like you have drawn back.

According to the study conducted by the Pew Research Center, 35-43% of job seekers during the Great Recession reported loss of contact with close friends. [14-1]

This is definitely not the time to withdraw and is, in fact, the time to step up. As a true friend, dear family member, or devoted spouse, this is the time your job seeker needs you the most. By reading the suggestions and comments from job seekers, you will better know how to handle the interaction with your job seeker. What you will see is that there are no magic words to say. Simply say, "I'm sorry you are going through this, I am here for you, what can I do?", and then be there for them.

There is no shame being in a job transition. In this new job market, most of us will be in a job transition again.

In the article "How to Comfort a Friend that has Lost a Corporate Job" by the Pew Research Center, step one suggests that if you hear a rumor that a friend or family member has lost their job, bring it up with them in private and say "I heard. I'm sorry." Then just listen. [14-2]

Do not treat the person as broken. Treat them as the person you know they can be. They are the same person they were when they were employed. Being upbeat shows your belief in them. [14-3]

Ask up front what type of conversations they want and when they want it. Keep the lines of communication open.

Be Intentional

Be intentional about keeping in touch with your job seeker often, perhaps even more often than ever before, while they are in a job transition. Do not act as if anything is wrong. Do not let any discomfort you feel keep you from being a good friend. Your turn to be in a job transition may come, and you will realize how important friends and family are.

Staying in touch does not always have to take the form of serious conversations about the job search. Staying in touch can also take the form of fun, relaxation, exercising, or any positive interaction.

Understandably, you are busy too with your own life and commitments. Time flies. To help you remember to stay in touch, so it is not weeks or months before you realize it, set a repeat reminder in your calendar so you remember to reach out via e-mail or phone and schedule times to get together in person on a regular basis.

Ask to meet them for lunch. Remember finances may be tight at this time so select a place that is affordable, maybe where you have a two-for-one coupon, or offer to pick up the tab and tell them they can return the favor when you are in your job search.

In the Voice of Job Seekers

The worst thing someone could do is not talk to me, find out how I am doing. I was surprised by my last layoff and the lack of contact with people. .... . This time can be very isolating for a lot of people. Some contact is always appreciated.

- Brian H.

Keep engaged with the unemployed person. Don't abandon them because you don't have the perfect words to fix their situation. That will only make things worse for them, exacerbating the feeling of being disconnected.

– Bruce S.

Worst thing: Avoid[ed] me because I was unemployed and my situation made them feel uncomfortable. Or, stop[ped] communicating and being a friend. Liked for people to do: Get together periodically... be a friend by helping to maintain the relationship and showing positivity and spiritual guidance or prayer. Just do things together. Be there for me to talk through things and empower me to step outside the box.

  – Teresa F.

..the worst thing a person could do (and did) was look at me with pity, like I was an 'outsider' with a contagious disease.

  - Janet C.

What I have done for my friends is encourage them to meet up for lunch. We have a great conversation and get caught up and they forget about the job search for a moment. Now I am currently the one undergoing a job search and they are returning the favor!

  - Yvonne N.

My friends and neighbors have treated me as if I have the plague and am highly contagious....I have felt very alone throughout it.

- Cindi L.

Worst: not respond to my e-mails.

- Roy S.

For a friend, keep in touch often so they know they are not forgotten. Being out of work can be isolating. ...Just someone sending an email to say hi counts for me. A friend in need is a friend indeed. Technology has not changed that!

- Darla W.

My friends are the best. They supported me with phone calls, e-mails...

- Susan F.

Worst: Changing plans that we set up together.

- Laura B.

Worst: [He/she] wasn't there.

- Carolyn B.

Worst: Ignore [what I was going through]

- Paul P.

Acknowledging the frustration of not finding a job and how hard you are working.

- Robin G.

Best: [Two] former managers were always available to talk when I needed someone to talk to who could relate to what I was dealing with. Worst thing - I would say learning that some people who I thought would be there for me were not, that was most disappointing, but it was also a learning experience.

– Peter W.

What is the worst thing someone did? Wasn't there.

– Carolyn B.

I think the worst thing someone can do is not getting back to a job seeker after they contact them to ask for advice, a link up or help. It's even worse if that someone has offered to help and didn't get back with you when you contacted them about it. I understand people are busy, but keeping your word is important, too. I also know for myself that the support and concern or help from anyone at a time like this is appreciated and will never be forgotten.

– Darla W.

With the exception of a couple of people, my friends (what few I had) and neighbors have treated me as if I have the plague and am highly contagious. I am a single woman, alone in Atlanta. My family is not close by and, even if they were, we are not a close knit family (even through this difficult economy.)

– Cindi L.

The worst is the people who don't return calls because they
are just too busy (working) and maybe just a little
uncomfortable. Unemployment isn't a transmittable disease
and this could be them but by the grace of God. It is really
disappointing to not get a response when you leave
messages. Many times I call people looking for information
that I need to help me but never hear back. I really don't
think they understand what that does to a person's self-
esteem. This too shall pass!
- Jim B.

Chapter Summary

Job seekers experience an increased sense of isolation
since they no longer have the human interaction provided by the
job. This is the time you need to step up and be intentional about
staying in touch.

Believer's Bonus

The Bible not only states that we should be there, but that we should step forward to go through this with them.

Carry each other's burdens, and in this way you will fulfill the law of Christ.

– Galatians 6:2

Be completely humble and gentle; be patient, bearing with another in love.

- Ephesians 4:2

Love your neighbor as yourself.

– Leviticus 19:18

Plans fail for lack of counsel, but with many advisers they succeed.

– Proverbs 15:22

A cheerful look brings joy to the heart, and good news gives health to the bones.

– Proverbs 15:30

"For where two or three come together in my name, there am I with them."

– Matthew 18:20

"Do to others as you would have them do to you."

– Luke 6:31

Do not be like the Pharisee that prayed about himself: "God I thank you that I am not like other men".

– Luke 18:11

Mourn with those who mourn.

- Romans 12:15

Be devoted to one another in brotherly love.

- Romans 12:10

Do not be proud, but be willing to associate with people of low position. Do not be conceited.

- Romans 12:16

Praise be to the God and Father of our Lord Jesus Christ, the Father of compassion and the God of all comfort, who comforts us in all our troubles, so that we can comfort those in any trouble with the comfort we ourselves have received from God.

– 2 Corinthians 1:3-4

For this reason, since the day we heard about you, we have not stopped praying for you and asking God to fill you with the knowledge of his will through all spiritual wisdom and understanding.

– Colossians 1:9

Therefore, as God's chosen people holy and dearly loved, clothe yourself with compassion, kindness, humility, gentleness, and patience. Bear with each other.

– Colossians 3:12-13

I urge, then, first of all, that requests, prayers, intercession and thanksgiving be made for everyone.

– 1 Timothy 2:1

If anyone does not provide for his relatives, and especially for his immediate family, he has denied the faith and is worse than an unbeliever.

– 1 Timothy 5:8

Let us hold unswervingly to the hope we profess, for he who promised is faithful. And let us consider how we may spur one another on toward love and good deeds. Let us not give up meeting together, as some are in the habit of doing, but let us

encourage one another.

– Hebrews 10:23-25

Anyone, then, who knows the good he ought to do and doesn't

do it, sins.

– James 4:17

Dear friends, since God so loved us, we also ought to love

another. No one has ever seen God, but if we love one another,

God lives in us and his love is made complete in us.

- 1 John 4:11-12

Chapter 15

Just Listen

In the job search, job seekers are drawing upon all of their energy to maintain a positive attitude. They must then have a place where they can honestly and openly share their frustrations and concerns. As you will see, many job seekers want a person to hear them, a place to vent. They are not always looking for someone to try to fix the problems; they sometimes are just looking for someone to listen. The opportunity to vent thoughts and frustrations gives the job seeker an outlet, and the process of venting makes them feel better. Remember, the best conversationalist is the one who really listens.

By listening, we do not mean just sit there while they talk. They have to feel heard. If you do not already know them, learn active listening techniques since these skills will serve you well in all aspects of your life. Actively listen to your job seeker so they feel they have been heard.

Venting versus Brainstorming

When I was a manager in the corporate world, I had a rule that when someone on my team wanted to come to talk, they had to let me know if they were just venting or wanted me to help with a solution. For those who were venting, the rule was that I would listen and once they left, there was nothing left for me to do (i.e. I would have done my part by listening, and I would take no action). If, however, they were coming in to talk and look for me to take action, then they had to come in with one realistic solution. By telling me up front what their goal was, I knew how to do my part. I actively listened either way, but I knew to turn off the solution finder side of my brain if they were only venting.

You may want to preface your interactions with your job seeker the same way if you have the tendency to jump in with solutions. Ask if they want to brainstorm or if they just want to vent. If they want to brainstorm, they should come with at least one realistic option to show they are not looking to you to make their life decisions. As a parent of an adult job seeker or even a young adult, you want to encourage them to generate their own options and own their decisions. That is how they grow, learning from their mistakes and celebrating their own successes.

As a job search coach, I have had clients who wanted me to tell them what career or company to choose. I make sure my clients know I am not making the decision. I will give my input and help draw out the pros and cons but they own the decision they make. You should encourage and allow them to make their own decisions as well.

Other Listening Tips

They may want to talk about the job search or they may want to talk about something else. Follow their lead.

Have empathy but do not go negative. Let them vent, but do not encourage self-pity. They should feel better afterward.

Do not have a look of pity, a long face or a sad voice.

Do not share ideas unless they ask or else they could read into it that you think they are incapable of handling it themselves.

If they propose an idea, do not shoot it down. It is not your job to play the devil's advocate unless they ask you to.

Having someone who just listens is important, as you will see in the comments below from job seekers.

In the Voice of Job Seekers

The best thing a friend, significant other, or parent ever did for me was listen, not look down on me, and most of all not ask the dreaded question every time they saw me "so, have you found a job yet" ... the best thing a person can do is listen (not try to fix the problem).

 - Janet C.

Be a good listener and solid person they can vent to. Ask open ended questions. Do not preach to them. Ask them if they would like help/advice/resources before you just forward it or tell them.

- Susan S.

Listen a LOT. Listen to what they're looking for. Don't assume. They may be ready for a career change or might want to continue in the same career. Listen to what THEY are looking for.

– Bruce S.

What would [I] have liked someone to do? Brainstorm with me.

- Deb H.

Best: Showing interest in the searcher's efforts, being a good listener to the woes, being open-minded to new work a searcher may consider, offering assistance when possible, or encouragement if not. Unemployed people would prefer to not be judged by others based on their sad employment situation. They are not alone and many did nothing to deserve this.

- Theresa W.

What is the worst: Ignore it. What would you have liked someone to do? Ask and listen. Oh, and pray.

– Paul P.

[It helps when they] Listen to all your weird ideas about changing careers or going back to school or becoming a nun or travelling around the world.

– Shelia M.

Chapter Summary

You play an important role in the job seeker's search by providing a place for them to go where someone listens and hears them. Learn and use active listening techniques.

Believer's Bonus

He who answers before listening – that is his folly and his shame.

- Proverbs 18:13

Everyone should be quick to listen, slow to speak

- James 1:19

Be still, and know that I am God.

- Psalm 46:10

Let the wise listen and add to their learning and let the

discerning get guidance

- *Proverbs 1:5*

Chapter 16

Support and Encourage

The ultimate goal is for the job seeker to find and land the right job for them. Your role and your desire in the process, as evidenced by you reading this book, is to provide the right environment and assistance for that to happen. Motivation comes from within the job seeker, but they must have an encouraging environment to nurture that motivation.

Encouragement vs. Intimidation

The job search takes longer now than ever before. Be patient and consistent in your support and encouragement.

There is a difference between encouragement and intimidation, both in the approach and in the results.

---

en cour age - verb

1. to inspire with courage, spirit, or confidence

2. to stimulate by assistance, approval, etc.

- Dictionary.com

---

in-tim-i-date – verb

1.   to make timid or fearful

2.   to compel or deter by or as if by threats

Synonyms: Browbeat, bully, cow

Intimidate implies inducing fear or sense of inferiority into another

Cow implies reduction to a state where the spirit is broken or all courage is lost

- Merriam-Webster

Be on guard not to be passive-aggressive. Nagging, pushing, ordering, and applying guilt are different approaches of intimidation used to get someone to do something. For job seekers who may already feel bad about themselves these approaches add negativity to an already negative time in their lives. It takes a good attitude to land that job; doing anything that makes the job seeker feel worse is counterproductive.

If you see your job seeker on the couch, in front of the TV, or playing computer games, do not jump to the conclusion that they have been goofing off all day and have not made any movement toward finding a job. They may be just taking a break. It would be like the boss at work seeing you talking to a coworker and assuming you have not been working.

If your job seeker says or does something that is negative or out of character you can say, "That is not like you to…" and then what they said or did. "You are better than that".

Praise and encourage all forward progress, not just the results. You now know the process and all that goes into the job search. You also know that progress is not based on the number of applications that have been submitted. Instead, encourage the job seeker especially when they are doing things out of their comfort zone such as networking.

How to be Encouraging

To be encouraging, be specific when you are offering comments. Just as the job seeker has to list details in the form of STARs to support their answers, having specifics in your feedback adds weight to your comments.

Remind the job seeker of the value they provide to employers and how smart they are. Remind them that they have a lot to offer an employer and recount their prior accomplishments.

This is just a transition, like going from one grade in school to another (just not as much fun). Remind them they have been in a life transition before and went through that successfully; they will be successful again. The job market changed; it is not them.

In other words, replace the 8-track tape that is playing negative thoughts in their heads with positive feedback, and remind them that you are there for them the whole way.

Consistency

You are going to see the word consistency in this book a lot. It is said that it takes from five to eight positive comments to replace one negative one. [16-1] If you are not consistent in your encouragement, it will take longer for the job seeker to know that they have your full support.

Some job seekers may try pushing people away. They may be doing this consciously or subconsciously. They may not feel they are deserving of this support, or they may be testing the friendship. Be patient and be consistent. Continuous drops of water can carve a rock.

Support

There are proactive actions you should take during the job seeker's transition. The emotional support and encouragement you provide should take the form of that identified by the job seeker using the book *The Five Languages* of *Appreciation in the Workplace* mentioned in Chapter 12.

It is okay if the job seeker declines your offers to help. There may be many reasons they are turning your offer down. They could be in denial about needing help. The job seeker may decline your help so they feel in control of some aspect of their life. Do not take offense if they do. Let them know the offer stands and continue to be there for them.

If their language of appreciation is affirmation, bring up previous accomplishments and assure them that even though the job market is very different and tough, they will find a job and the company will be lucky to have them.

If the language of appreciation is receiving gifts, a gift card for gas or groceries may be appreciated. Another idea is a gift certificate for dinner for two, for the job seeker and spouse, and offering to baby-sit their kids. Offering to babysit the kids is also helpful so they can attend networking meetings or just have time alone with their spouse.

If quality time is the language of appreciation, schedule some time on the weekend to do something you both consider fun, allowing the job seeker to get away from the job search and get out enjoying the day.

For job seekers who have the language of appreciation of physical touch, a reassuring touch on the arm, a hug, or a pat on the back may be welcomed.

If you are good at editing, offer to proofread their documents before they send them out. If you are good at interviewing, offer to conduct a mock interview.

Brainstorm with them solutions to eliminate obstacles the person has encountered. Remember, brainstorming is a process where all people share ideas without judgment; it is not you telling them how to do it.

If the job seeker is exploring other careers or industries, support their efforts; encourage this exploration. Give the job seeker room to be creative. Do not impose your own expectations, dreams, or standards upon them. They have *their own* life with *their own* dreams and desires. If your job seeker usually makes sound decisions, then they are capable of making them now, too. You must be optimistic while they consider seeking their passion or changing directions.

Moving In

If a job seeker moves in with you, be it an adult child moving back in with parents (referred to as the boomerang generation [16-2]), parents moving in with their adult children, or a friend moving in with another, all parties have to be in agreement on what the arrangement will be. [16-3] According to the answer posted online on this topic, if an adult child moves back in with parents, then both parents have to be in agreement

on how it is going to work. If you need to get a third party to
help with the negotiations, then do it. 16-4

The ground rules should include who is paying for what
and who is doing what. The job seeker needs to be treated as an
adult. Setting house rules and requiring them to participate in
the household chores and expenses actually helps increase their
self-esteem. 16-5

In the Voice of Job Seekers

Share your experience and encourage him or her.
– Mantosh P.

The best things: Focus on the positive... Encourage us to get
out from behind the computer/ [or out] of the house and
network with people.
– Ed H.

The best thing my sister said to me was how good I was at
my job; that I have great people skills and someone should be

breaking down the door to hire me. In other words, she made me feel like I was worth something, to someone, again. Comments like that can get me through a very bad day of rejection e-mails and no call-backs. I'm a very independent person, but what I need more than anything right now is emotional support.

- Monselle V.

Some of the best things a friend or parent can do for you is offer support. That is the best thing my parents have offered me since I have been through two layoffs.

- Brian H.

It is very important to have a good support system when someone is out of work. The support system can be for monetary reasons or purely an emotional support. Most of the time[the] job seeker's unstated need [is]to be supported emotionally.

– Suresh V.

The best thing is the support and encouragement that I could succeed with my change!

– Matt F.

Acknowledge the frustration of not finding a job and how hard you are working.

– Robin G.

I have numerous friends who offer words of encouragement particularly friends who are currently going through the same process or have recently obtained new careers. Support and words of encouragement are the greatest gift an individual can give (and maybe money if you are in need of financials resources to get by) a job seeker!!

– Al F.

Understanding moments I need support AND moments I need time for me.

– Laura B.

The best thing that friends, spouse, or parents can do is, to trust [in] you, give moral support to you.

– Rahul S.

What I would like: I ask friends and family to have confidence in me and faith in God and to remind me why they have confidence in me when I get discouraged.

– Diana B.

My friends are the best. They supported me with phone calls, e-mails, meals, one of my friends sold me her laptop for a cheap, cheap price (I wouldn't let her give it to me), provided computer support when I needed it, listened to me and consoled me when I was down. They passed my résumé along - which in the end is how I got my job. One of my friends gave me a calling card so I wouldn't have to use all my cell phone minutes. They didn't judge me; they helped. Then they celebrated with me when I got the job! I couldn't have asked for anything more.

– Susan F.

Best thing- A couple of friends did not wait for me to ask if I needed financial help, they just gave without asking if I needed anything. I will remember them the rest of my life. A few friends have been faithful to send an e-mail or call and say "I love you, and God loves you, and YOU are in my prayers"- and I know they meant every word. Reminds me of the country song by Tim McGraw, Tracy Lawrence, Kenny Chesney "You Find Out Who Your Friends Are."
– Greg H.

I would have liked friends, family and neighbors to let me know that it will all turn out all right. I know that I am not the only one struggling during this economy; however, I have felt very alone throughout it.
– Cindi L.

The best: they told me not to give up. I will find something that I would like to do.
– Lynn F.

Pray for me and my job search.

– Roy S.

Chapter Summary

The job seeker needs your consistent support and encouragement. Inspire them and provide a positive environment so they believe in themselves and have courage to face the job search.

Believer's Bonus

The best thing you can do to support your job seeker is to pray for them regularly. You can rest in the assurance that God has a plan for them and He is in control. Pray that God will provide you the right words at the right time to keep them encouraged.

May the Lord answer you when you are in distress; …May he give you the desires of your heart and make all your plans succeed. We will shout for joy when you are victorious…May the Lord grant you all your requests.

- *Psalm 20:1–5*

"Come to me, all who are weary and burdened, and I will give you rest".

- *Matthew 11:28*

Never be lacking in zeal, but keep your spiritual fervor, serving the Lord. Be joyful in hope, patient in affliction, faithful in prayer.

- *Romans 12:11-13*

We have different gifts, according to the grace given us. … if it is encouraging, let him encourage…

- *Romans 12:6-8*

Praise be to the God and Father of our Lord Jesus Christ, the Father of compassion and the God of all comfort, who comforts us in all our troubles, so that we can comfort those in any trouble with the comfort we ourselves have received from God.

- 2 Corinthians 1:3-4

Carry each other's burdens, and in this way you will fulfill the law of Christ.

- Galatians 6:2

Let us hold unswervingly to the hope we profess, for he who promised is faithful. And let us consider how we may spur one another on toward love and good deeds. Let us not give up meeting together, as some are in the habit of doing, but let us encourage one another.

- Hebrews 10:23-25

Now faith is being sure of what we hope for and certain of what we do not see.

– Hebrews 11:1

Chapter 17

Provide Valuable Input

You know a lot about your job seeker. In order to sell their talents and get hired, job seekers must identify their competitive advantage: the traits, skills, and prior accomplishments that make them unique and communicate the relevance to the company's needs. You can help them recall their previous accomplishments and unique skills.

As humans, we all tend to minimize the skills and traits that come easy to us. We think that because it is easy for us, it can't be anything special. The truth is that others admire us for these skills and wish they were as good at them.

You can help your job seeker by reminding them of their unique skills, abilities, and previous accomplishments. You do not have to wait to be asked before offering up this information; it will help the job seeker's self-confidence to be reminded of what makes them special.

As mentioned before, accomplishments should be listed in STAR format. STAR stands for **S**ituation or **T**ask that they faced, the **A**ctions they took, and the **R**esults they received. A form has been provided in Appendix A that you can complete and give to your job seeker.

In the Voice of Job Seekers

> *The best thing that a friend did was sit me down and help me identify my skills and how I could use them in a different way.*
>
> *– Liz H.*

> *I went to my family and friends to gain their insights to my characteristics and their perception of my abilities. This was helpful for me. Their responses were positive and reassuring. It is the reassurance that you are worthwhile and that it is*

the situation, not your performance, that is the problem. I

needed that reassurance because each day I send out résumés

and get so few responses. It takes a toll on your self-worth

over time.

- Phillip D.

A few of my former coworkers posted recommendations for

me on LinkedIn without me even asking. That meant a lot to

me; I really appreciated it.

– Lydia B.

Encourage them as to how they are qualified for other things.

- Eric S.

When my dealership closed, one of the most helpful tools

they left me with was a letter of recommendation with the

company letterhead on top, signed by all the Service

Department managers.

- Nick A.

Best: tell all their friends that you are looking, and point out

your wonderful qualifications. Support your decision not to

take the first job that comes along if you know it isn't right.

– Shelia M.

Chapter Summary

You are aware of your job seeker's unique qualities that

they may not see for themselves. Share those insights and it will

help your job seeker sell themselves.

Believer's Bonus

I praise you because [the job seeker is] fearfully and wonderfully

made; your works are wonderful, I know that full well.

- Psalm 139:14

We have different gifts, according to the grace given us. If a man's

gift is prophesying, let him use it in proportion to his faith. If it is serving, let him serve; if it is teaching, let him teach; if it is encouraging, let him encourage; if it is contributing to the needs of others, let him give generously; if it is leadership, let him govern diligently; if it is showing mercy, let him do it cheerfully.

- *Romans 12:6-8*

Chapter 18

Leverage Your Network

As you now realize, networking is the best and most productive way to find a job. It allows people to build trust through a common interest whether through an industry, job responsibility, or hobby.

In this area, you can do a lot to help your job seeker. You may not have a job to offer but you know people. Actively help the job seeker connect with people you know. Unless you ask, you may not even realize that people you know can help. Remind the job seeker of the people they know who can help.

To help the job seeker network, you have to know how to network yourself. Learning how to network will help you too.

Regardless if the person is an extrovert or introvert, they may not be comfortable striking up conversations with people they do not know. Like many things we do though, it is just a matter of learning how to do it and then practicing it until it becomes more natural. If you are not a good networker or want to improve, there is a list of recommended books in the back of this book that are great resources on the topic of networking.

Ask your job seeker for their completed Networking Guide (a template of the Networking Guide is provided in Appendix B). It includes the various titles of the position the job seeker is pursuing and their target companies. Place the completed Networking Guide on your refrigerator or someplace where you will see it on a regular basis.

When you are at parties or other events, find out if anyone has a contact at any of the target companies. Even if your contact does not work in the same field the job seeker is pursuing, it is still helpful for the job seeker to meet so they can gather information that will be helpful in the search. If you hear anyone say they are hiring for one of the positions, introduce that person to your job seeker.

With their permission, take your job seeker's Networking Guide to people in your network to see if they know anyone who can connect your job seeker to anyone within one of the target companies.

Also tell your job seeker about any networking groups you hear about. Do not forget to preface it with "You may already know about this group..." so that you do not insult them by telling them something they already know.

Social Networking

Social Networking is the process of using programs on the Internet to stay in touch with other people. You are probably familiar with Facebook, which facilitates personal connections. As mentioned in the chapter on marketing materials, the most powerful social networking program for business connections is LinkedIn.

Job seekers must have a LinkedIn profile. It will help your job seeker if you also create a LinkedIn profile, connect to members of your network, and invite your job seeker to connect to you.

For more information on LinkedIn and the uses for networking, a list of resources is available in Appendix C.

In the Voice of Job Seekers

A friend put me in contact with someone who just successfully completed a 9 month job search. The one hour I spent with him, learning what works and did not work, saved me weeks/months from my job search. Another friend he put me in contact with a seasoned networker who put me in contact with more seasoned networkers, etc.

– Jim M.

The people I cherished the most [during the search] were the people that truly knew the word 'network' and how to use it.
– Janet C.

One thing I did was ask my professors in college if they had any connections they would help me get introduced to. That was before LinkedIn, and guess what, it worked!
- Susan S.

[The best thing was] friends who look for and share job leads without being asked, then offering to be references.
- Steve B.

When I went through a job transition, the support of close people was key. We started a group at church to help people on their spiritual walk to learn from the process. If you listen it is amazing what God is teaching you through the process. It can strengthen relationships with God, spouse and others or it can pull you apart, it just depends on how you grasp the situation!

– Todd B.

One of the best things that someone has done for me is to insist that I attend a Christian based job networking group. I was suffering from depression and could not bounce back. I needed that weekly support of people just showing me that they wanted good for me. The depression symptoms are gone and I have moved on. I had realized early on that being fired or being in a reduction in force was sort of like death of a close friend. I was expecting those feelings and yet, I could not leave them behind. Once I went to RUMC [Roswell United Methodist Church; Roswell, Georgia] and the other churches that I have attended, I have been able to let go and move on. Before that I was stuck in the bad part of the cycle.

– Charlie B.

Point me towards the Faith Based networking groups sooner in my search. Once I found them, I was more at peace, because I had others who understood what I was going

through.

- Jim B.

In addition to connecting them, however, mentoring or

training them in the process can be beneficial as well. I am a

job seeker right now, transitioning from [one industry to

another], and I have had to develop these new skills, which

honestly felt foreign at first. I'm guessing there are a lot of

other job seekers out there who would love experienced

networkers to take them under their wings and show them

the ropes--not only that, but also to show them how to

minister in Christ's name through these networking

relationships.

– Scott F.

The best thing for me with my job search was to join

networking groups. It put me right into a peer group of

people in the same spot as me. It took the edge off the strong

emotions that otherwise came out at home (either alone at

home or with my family). My friend gave me a great

metaphor from physics: it takes more effort as a boxer to

throw a punch and not connect with their opponent, than it

does to throw and land a punch. Since so much of job

seeking is swinging at air, the thing that helped me the most

was all the stuff that had nothing to do with looking for

work. House projects. Volunteer work. Artistic endeavors.

They all fell into the area where I could land a punch. It was

so important to "connect". The worst was getting a lead

from a networking colleague and reaching out and not

hearing back from the person I was referred to (or try to

schedule an in person [meeting] and then not having things

come to fruition). That was worse than sending out résumés

with no response. It got my hope up too much.

-Symantha G.

I think helping job seekers network is a HUGE help! We

may not know of a specific job opportunity, but we can

leverage our relationships to sponsor introductions to

facilitate the job seeker's networking. Most people find a job through who they know...
– Lisa L.

Worst thing people did... not understanding networking. I got no help when I asked for leads even though I knew they knew people who would be useful. I would like introductions to other people. The people who I would think understood networking did not understand it even when I explained it.
– Laura B.

Putting them in contact with your network is also very helpful (finding an occasion, or creating one not related to job search, is better).
- Guillaume P.

Best thing: Be proactive. If someone you know is seeking employment make sure they're LinkedIn and connected to networking groups. Help them get networked and know what they CAN do, what they WANT to do and what they're WILLING to do. This will make you a strong "link".

Worst thing: Asked a connection to offer contact assistance

to someone in my network. They "could not help" because

the company was in transition. What I would have liked:

That person to say, "Things are in transition but let's get

connected and see where it goes".

- Phil P.

Sending them obvious jobs any seeker would find is to imply

they are not looking.

– Eric S.

Network, network, network. I have several relatives and dear

friends who are out of work and they don't know the first

thing about networking. Every encounter is an opportunity

to make a connection for the future. Anyone who wants to be

helpful should:

1. *Offer to review the résumé*

2. *Give honest feedback and helpful suggestions*

3. *Introduce them to good connections*

4.   Reach out to your closest contacts for help

5.   Use social media to give them exposure

6.   Teach them social media if they aren't using it

But you should NOT:

1.   Schedule meetings for them (they may not be interested)

2.   Claim they have skills they don't

3.   Recommend them if they might reflect badly on you

4.   Give your contact private information about them

- Kathi B.

Best: Friends and family letting people in their personal and professional life know that you are looking for work. Asking the people in their network if they know of companies hiring or other contacts that may help provide insight through information[al] meetings. Friends inside companies who put your résumé into the hands of a hiring party or HR recruiter when your qualifications match an open position.

– Diana B.

Friends and family should be acting as a team to assist job seekers. By that I mean actively looking at internal job boards where they work, carrying your résumé to the right person, introducing you to the "right people" for networking opportunities, and telling you to "hang in there" when things look bad.

- Judy C.

I found my answers in the networking groups, some have been so nice to me. It is so difficult out in the world today. I am a single parent so I don't have a lot of support except when I go to the networking groups. I am hoping that all the action that I have done and will continue to do will bring me a wonderful opportunity. I have helped a lot of people and I am sure God will take care of me.

– Lynn F.

Worst? Agree to present my résumé to someone in the company then wimp out.

– Shelia M.

For an acquaintance, the best thing [in my opinion] is to keep your ears open and let them know if you hear of an opening or lead. For a friend, do the same and keep in touch often so they know they aren't forgotten about. Being out of work can be isolating. For a close friend, do all of the above plus take them to lunch or dinner here and there (for example) or whatever someone is comfortable with. I think the closer the relationship, the more time you would want to invest in offering support, reassurance and an ear. Oh and hugs are nice, too!

– Darla W.

Inquire about what I[was] looking for, connect on LinkedIn, and offer some websites to look [at].

- Fatima G.

What would you have liked someone to do? Mentoring.

– Laura B.

Chapter Summary

You can do a lot to help your job seeker by helping them network with your contacts and connect to your LinkedIn network. If you do not already know how to, you may want to learn how to network (social networking and in person). It is another skill that is essential in today's world.

Believer's Bonus

Plans fail for lack of counsel, but with many advisers they succeed.

- *Proverbs 15:22*

And things you have heard me say in the presence of many witnesses entrust to reliable men who will also be qualified to teach others.

- *2 Timothy 2:2*

Chapter 19

Know What to Say and What Not to Say

No one intentionally says the wrong thing to someone they care about. Normally, a misspoken word comes from emotion or not understanding the impact these words have on the other person. For instance, when you try to assure them that it is the economy and not something that they have done personally, saying "you're not alone" in fact feels to the job seeker that you are trying to diminish their pain as if they do not have the right to hurt like they do.

You will see a trend in the following comments from job seekers; the words not to say have to do with being put down or with having brought to light what could be perceived as a failure. Conversely, the words to say are uplifting to the person, encouraging them and reminding them of their value and strengths.

Styles of Communication

As you probably have already discovered, men and women communicate differently. [19-1] People of the same gender also have different communication styles. Some people prefer all of the details while others prefer the bottom line or sound bites. Find out which style your job seeker prefers and let them know which you prefer.

Do Not Kick a Man (or Woman) While They are Down

Words are very powerful. Putting down a person whose self-confidence has already been rattled does not help the job seeker's attitude. Without a positive attitude, the job seeker is not going to get a job.

There are a few people in this world who believe you kick a person who is on the ground with a broken leg and yell at them to get up as a form of motivation. This approach is not one of motivation but fear. Fear is not a long-term motivation that inspires. Fear does not add to a person's self-confidence, and although you may get some initial movement, any progress that results will not be sustained and the fear can irreparably damage the relationship you have with this person. [19-2]

Just like a fort in the pioneer days, if a person is under attack, they will close up. Only when a person (like the fort) feels safe from attack will they open up.

How to Ask a Job Seeker How They are Doing

Over the years, many job seekers have shared with me that they wished people would simply ask, "How are you?" or "How is your day going?" or "How can I help you with job leads?"

Although well intended, asking details about the job search may put the job seeker in the position of feeling like a failure by having to share updates that are less than positive. As you will see in the comments provided by the job seekers, "Have you had any interviews?", "Why is it taking so long to find a job? and "How is the job search going?" can be dreaded questions to someone in the job search. It is the equivalent of asking a single person "Why aren't you married yet?" which can be interpreted as "What is wrong with you?" It is best to use "how" questions instead of "what" questions, and never show pity in your tone when you ask. [19-3]

- If in doubt, when you are told by a person that they have lost their job, the simplest reply is to sincerely say "I'm sorry. What can I do for you?" and then listen and follow through.

- Certain phrases should not be used. Example "If you were working..." implies the person is not trying to find a job.

- Do not compare your job seeker to others.

- Talk about the person's good qualities, complimenting them on something specific and making special note of positive things that they do.

- Do not ask a million questions.

- Do not deliver lectures.

- Other than in the case of a spouse, do not share your fears for them.

- Learn interpersonal skills, especially those for handling conflict. An example is how to use "I" statements instead of "you" statements. [19-4]

- Stifle the urge to blame, nag, or push. That does not help; it only makes everything worse.

- Agree to keep blaming and negativity out of conversations during the job transition.

- Do not give constructive criticism at this time unless they specifically ask you for it.

In the Voice of Job Seekers

What to say and not say in the words of job seekers:

[Worst thing is] just being insensitive, saying that "people who can't find a job just aren't trying hard enough, or are lazy".

– Christine

The worst thing is to tell me that I am too old for a job. I would have liked someone to tell me that there is a job out there no matter how old I am and not to give up. And if you can dream it, it will happen to you.

– Mary T.

Things [said by] well-meaning people that sometimes grate on me: "How long have you been out of work?" I really don't need to be reminded. Or asking after an interview, "How did it go?" I won't know how it went until I learn whether or not I've been called back or hired. I'd much rather hear "I was praying for you or thinking about you today." [Another bad thing is] asking the question, "How could they have let you go?" I've been wondering that

myself. When you've been a strong performer in your

position and let go because of budget reasons, it's sometimes

a thin line between staying positive and dropping into

depression.

– Steve B.

The worst things [people do]: start every conversation with

"So how's your job search going?"; insist on focusing on the

negative (e.g., bad market, other people's job search horror

stories); forward our résumés to people without telling me.

– Ed H.

The worst thing someone can do is to put down a person

who is searching for a job in this economy by implying they

are lazy or worthless, not being a good provider for their

family. Some people do fit that description, but that would

have been evident prior to their current situation so people

should remember that fact and act accordingly to reinforce positive thoughts for that person since they are probably

generating enough of their own negative feelings.

– Theresa W.

[From a recruiter] *Other worse things: Telling the candidate they'll*

never get the job because they're not good enough (resulting in an

insecure and shy candidate). Telling the candidate they walk on water

and the company should beg on bended knee to hire them (resulting

in an arrogant candidate).

– Deb H.

Do NOT prattle on with the pseudo-assurance, "I'm sure

you'll find something in no time!" Sounds encouraging but

sets the bar high and implies there is something wrong with

the job seeker if he/she does NOT quickly find something.

It's annoying -- not helpful at all.

- Kevin Q.

Another networker who endured a longer unemployment got

in my face three times and each time blasted "There are no jobs." As true or false as this may be, I must suffer under the illusion that I will find and take a position.

   – Carolyn B.

The Worst: The negative talk that the economy is so bad that I should just take any kind of job.

– Lynn F.

Make the statement, "You haven't found a job yet?!"

   – Fatima G.

Avoid questions like: "What are you going to do if you don't find anything ?"

- Guillaume P.

Worst: A parent saying, "I can't sleep, I'm sick to my stomach. I think you're going to go bankrupt and lose your home."

– Diana B.

What I hated was being told constantly that "When one door closes, another opens". That may be true and intellectually I may know it, but it is hell sitting out in the hall waiting.

- Marianne G.

Tell me what you like about me, that you believe in me, and you will do something to help me, and not just say you will do something. The question "What can I do to help you?" shows real love, compassion, and a person that actually cares. Knowing that someone is willing to bear the burden with us and walk with us when we need them the most is the most important thing, and means so much to us, more than that person will ever know, until they face the loss of a job. I think it only takes one or two times at the most to show someone what it feels like, and then they get it. Then, that person will realize all of the difficulties we have on a daily [and] weekly basis as we watch others go off to work, or take vacations, go to ball games, life goes on for them, as it should, so we really need support while we are watching others live their lives. It is no longer "business as usual" for us during this particular season of life.

- Greg H.

Just ask how I'm doing and really listen.

– Roy S.

The worst thing was someone telling me I know of no one who can help you. The best thing was someone asking me to tell them what I needed so they could help.

- Pat B.

The best thing for me is to hear from others who are in my position that they had been praying for me. That is such a lift to know that people care that much. It is also great when you can talk to others in this predicament and listen to what they have to say or maybe even look for things for them. It really feels good to help someone.

– Jim B.

One of the worst things that people do is go on and on about how much money I am losing each day. As if I do not feel each cent as I spend it. Dwelling on this subject is not a good thing to do. I am not talking about how to save money; I am talking about just repeating over and over that it must be tough to be out of work because you are spending all your savings.

– Charlie B.

The worst thing someone said to me while I was looking for a job is that I would never be able to get one since I've been unemployed for almost a year. [This "friend" said] that I'd be better off just getting a job in [retail] because that's all I would be qualified for.

– Ilene L.

Chapter Summary

There are things you should say: things that build the person up and show you care. There are things you should avoid saying: things that put the job seeker down or make them feel

worse about themselves. Being aware of these and saying the

right things will help you create a more positive environment in

which the job seeker will succeed.

Believer's Bonus

Just a reminder: When sharing your faith, scriptures, and

God's love, do it with humility as one of God's children to

another of His children. If you sound spiritually superior, it will

turn the other person off.

A man finds joy in giving an apt reply – and how good is a timely

word.

- Proverbs 15:23

Do not let any unwholesome talk come out of your mouths, but only what is helpful for building others up according to their needs, that it may benefit those who listen.

- Ephesians 4:29

May the words of my mouth and the meditation of my heart be pleasing in your sight, O Lord.

- Psalm 19:14

Refrain from anger and turn from wrath; do not fret – it leads only to evil.

- Psalm 37:8

A gentle answer turns away wrath, but a harsh word stirs up anger.

- Proverbs 15:1

The tongue that brings healing is a tree of life but a deceitful tongue crushes the spirit.

- Proverbs 15:4

The lips of the wise spread knowledge; not so the hearts of fools.

- Proverbs 15:7

The discerning heart seeks knowledge, but the mouth of a fool feeds on folly.

- Proverbs 15:14

A hot-tempered man stirs up dissension, but a patient man calms a quarrel.

- Proverbs 15:18

The heart of the righteous weighs its answers, but the mouth of the wicked gushes evil.

- Proverbs 15:28

A cheerful look brings joy to the heart, and good news gives health to the bones.

- *Proverbs 15:30*

The wise in heart are called discerning, and pleasant words promote instruction.

- *Proverbs 16:21*

A fool finds no pleasure in understanding but delights in airing his own opinions.

- *Proverbs 18:2*

He who guards his mouth and his tongue keeps himself from calamity.

- *Proverbs 21:23*

"Men will have to give account on the day of judgment for every careless word they have spoken."

- *Matthew 12:36*

"The good man brings good things out of the good stored up in his heart, and the evil man brings evil things out of the evil stored up in his heart. For out of the overflow of his heart his mouth speaks."

- *Luke 6:45*

Fathers, do not exasperate your children; instead bring them up in the training and instruction of the Lord.

- *Ephesians 6:4*

Chapter 20

Other Creative Ideas

The job seekers who responded to the poll provided some fantastic examples of creative things people did for them in their job search. The ideas included are just some examples. Let your creativity, resources, knowledge of your job seeker, and the circumstances lead you. When you come up with a new idea, please have your job seeker submit their story using the web site listed in the back of this book. The ideas may be included in updates and future editions of this book.

You can offer to help, but if they decline your help, respect and accept their "no".[20-1] Just let them know the offer still stands and continue to be there for them.

Provide discreet practical assistance. In a show I saw once, I was impressed by the gentle tactic the female character used to give someone an item without making the other person feel it was charity. The lady said she had bought more than she needed, and if the other person would take the excess off her hands, they would be doing her a favor. That is putting the receiver in the position of being the helper. Be discrete and gentle in your assistance to others.

When planning events, you want to keep in mind that job seekers cannot spend money like they did previously. You do not need to always pay for the job seeker's dinners or tickets; instead, plan events that do not cost as much or find ways where the job seeker can be responsible for an aspect of the event, such as doing the driving.

Invite the job seeker and family over for a cookout, and make the job seeker responsible for bringing the games.

Offer the family gift certificates for a dinner and movie.

If your neighbor or friend is unemployed, take them a meal they would enjoy (and keep in mind your vegetarian friends).

Share opportunities that you have available to you. If you know about a conference and are going, invite the job seeker to come along.

Other ideas included babysitting or paying for training or coaching. Be creative and thoughtful.

In the Voice of Job Seekers

I was offered an appointment with a career consultant - but didn't take it up, as I didn't think I needed it...and now part of my work is career coaching. It would have been good if I had understood how valuable career coaching could be at the time I was making big changes.

– Liz H.

A friend from church gave me a $100 gift card for a local grocery store ... which I stretched into lasting for three

months using sales, coupons and just being very frugal.
Food was a thoughtful gift, since we all need to eat. And a
gift card allowed me to select the food that I wanted and
needed.

- Christine

"Adopt" 5 unemployed [friends]. .. Make calls on their
behalf. Track down leads for them. Make referral calls for
them.

– Bruce S.

The class I took regarding using the Internet to land your
next job, taught me a lot about LinkedIn resources.

– Mary T.

A buddy [would] treat me [to] an occasional round of golf
and talk about anything but my job search.

- Steve B.

Best things: Be supportive -- sometimes with [money], sometimes with time. Babysitting kids, helping with industry research, helping with interviewing coaching, proofreading résumés and cover letters. Introducing you to others who may be able to help you. Playing an effective virtual secretary when key phone calls come in.
– Deb H.

During my job search that started back in 2002 (which lasted about a year), my parents paid for our vacation at a beach condo. It was a chance for me and my wife to get away (with minimal expense) and spend time focusing on our relationship. Things can become strained in a marriage when there is an extended search going on.
- Buck T.

Gave me an escape. I vented and unwound. It was an extremely difficult time. After the escape for a few days, I was able to return and breathe in and out almost normally.
– Carolyn B.

Small acts of kindness (lunch, etc.), monetary gift, and introducing me to contacts to network.

– Fatima G.

I have a friend that is looking for a job. I gave him a Starbucks card and told him to take people there for informational interviews. When he has an interview, I put money on the card so he can offer to buy...and if the person objects, he can say that he has a "coach" that's funding their get-together.

- Buck T.

My nephew will graduate this summer and he is starting his job search. He hates going shopping with his Mom (that's somewhat normal), so I offered to take him shopping (with his Mom's money) and buy him an interview suit. I combined it with a suit-buying trip for myself so we were actually shopping together but separate (you get the idea). This way I could advise him but also ask him for his advice on my suit. It worked well. It's important for college grads to see themselves as adults during this job searching process...and sometimes it's easier to get help from people other than Mom.

- Buck T.

What would I have liked? ...I would have liked it if there had been a support group for people who were dealing with specific issues I dealt with that few people in job search have to deal with. I have been able to deal with them in other ways, but a support group would have been nice.

– Peter W.

When I was out of work last time, some folks gave me some money and I felt that some could not afford it. Others would see that I was included in family events and that my share was covered.

– Laura B.

Best: took me out to lunch and paid for my lunch! Said I

could return the favor when I got a job.

– Patty F.

When my hairdresser found out I was in job search she said

it is critical that you are confident and presenting your best

self during your search. She insisted that I come in every 6-

8 weeks for a haircut and color and told me that she would

not take a penny for her services. I have been her customer

for 18 years and she said that she wasn't going to have me

worrying about presenting my best self and looking my

best. It was the most generous gift of pure caring and

selflessness that anyone has ever given me. I think about it

often and it reminds me daily to give of myself to others

and share my gifts.

– Barbara B.

When I was in a job search without steady income, we

tightened our belts in a number of ways. One was to

eliminate the "eat out" budget. However, a weekly

restaurant outing can be a great family time to recharge. So

we really missed that time when the income was not

coming in. So when a friend took us to dinner, it was a

huge blessing! So take a job seeking friend or family out to

dinner!

– Ken C.

Advice on CV [résumé] and cover letters are good.

- *Guillaume P.*

Chapter Summary

It is the thought that counts so put some thought into

ways to give or help your job seeker that they would find

affirming.

If you are able, be thoughtful and creative in ways to take

some pressure off your job seeker, giving them fun times,

helping with job search expenses, and showing in small ways

that you care.

If your job seeker declines your offer, let them know your offer stands and continue to stay in touch, continue to listen, and make your network available to them. In those ways, you are still helping.

Believer's Bonus

"Be careful not to do your 'acts of righteousness' before men, to be seen by them. If you do, you will have no reward from your Father in heaven. So when you give to the needy, do not announce it with trumpets…so that your giving may be in secret. Then your Father, who sees what is done in secret, will reward you."

- *Matthew 6:1-2, 4*

In everything I did, I showed you that by this kind of hard work we must help the weak, remembering the words the Lord Jesus himself said, "It is more blessed to give than to receive".

- *Acts 20:35*

Never be lacking in zeal, but keep your spiritual fervor, serving the Lord. Be joyful in hope, patient in affliction, faithful in prayer. Share with God's people who are in need.

- *Romans 12:11-13*

We have different gifts, according to the grace given us. If a man's gift ...is contributing to the needs of others, let him give generously.

- *Romans 12:6-8*

Carry each other's burdens, and in this way you will fulfill the law of Christ.

- *Galatians 6:2*

And whatever you do, whether in word or deed, do it all in the name of the Lord Jesus, giving thanks to God the Father through him.

- *Colossians 3:17*

Chapter 21

The Job Search Spouse

The husband and wife team of Geoff and Luann Wiggins lead a workshop for job seekers and their spouses. As they say, "When one spouse is unemployed, the family is unemployed".

21-1

The first thing couples need to do when one or the other spouse (or sadly in some cases, both) becomes unemployed is to process the loss and then develop a strategy and contingency plans.

The worst thing a spouse can do is act as if the job seeker needs to resolve the issue by themself. That is not a marriage.

The temporary experience of a job transition can result in increased love for each other. You can grow close together as you survive this ordeal. [21-2]

"Fasten Your Seat Belts; It is Going to be a Bumpy Ride"

When interviewing spouses for this book, one spouse said the thing they wanted most was a seat belt. I had expected to hear more tangible things such as time or attention. Instead, the thing this spouse wanted most was a way to more smoothly handle the ups and downs of the job search.

Interestingly enough, many job seekers tell me that they do not share with their spouse everything that is happening in order to buffer them from the ups and downs; they do not want to increase their spouse's anxiety. Job seekers go so far out of their way to buffer the spouse that some have been known to pretend to go to work so they do not have to tell their spouse that they lost their job. Let your spouse know how much information you want and need to feel included but not anxious.

As this Betty Davis line in the 1950 film "All About Eve" indicates, the job search can be a very bumpy ride with as many dramatic ups and downs as a roller coaster. The job search not only affects the emotions of your job seeker; your emotions will be affected as well.

If the relationship is rocky to begin with, the job loss can increase the stress. You are taking the right steps by reading this book to understand the new job market and what your spouse needs to do to succeed. You also need to take care of yourself, your family, and your relationship.

Process Your Own Loss

The loss of the job limits the family income, and the family income can impact life's essentials (home, utilities, food, transportation). Therefore, the deepest rooted fears or previous painful circumstances can come to light. You need to give yourself permission and take the time to process the loss you feel.

Next: Understand How Your Spouse Ticks

You and your spouse are wired differently; you have personality traits that drive behaviors and approaches to life. It helps any relationship (personal and business) to understand the other person. If you have not done so before, now is the perfect time to understand how your spouse ticks and vice versa.

Personality

There are various personality assessments you can take: Myers-Briggs, Jung, and others.

One of the personality traits identified is how the person gets their energy. Some people, referred to as extroverts, gain energy by being around people. They do not necessarily have to be the life of the party, although some are. They do, though, need to be around others or they get drained or start to climb the walls.

On the other hand, introverts do not get their energy by being around others; in fact, doing so drains their energy. It does not mean these people are shy (although some introverts tend to have shy tendencies). Being an introvert means the person must have time alone after being around others. Most people who have just met me do not believe it, but it is true: I am an introvert. Although I make presentations to rooms of hundreds of people, and enjoy doing so, I have to be alone afterwards to recharge my batteries.

We had an unusual snow storm in the Atlanta area in 2011 which closed the city down for days starting on a Monday. [21-3] When I spoke in the Atlanta area shortly after the storm, I could tell who is an extrovert; they are the ones who said they had to get out of the house by Tuesday (even though it was unsafe to do so). On the other hand, we introverts were fine the entire week as long as we had power and our supplies did not run out.

If you have an introvert spouse who has just been out networking, he or she will be drained and want to be alone for a while when they get home.

If you have an extrovert spouse and they have been home most of the day, they will want to go out and do something the minute you get home from whatever you were doing.

You will want to understand your personality and your spouse's. Agree on how to handle the differences. For example, if you want your introvert spouse to talk with you or help out around the house when they get home from a networking meeting, give them time alone to recharge first. Once they have recharged, they can interact with you and other family members and help out around the house. Conversely, if you are an introvert and work outside of the house and your extrovert job seeker has been home, consider giving them something they can do for you outside the house (run to pick up dinner or groceries) while you are recharging your battery.

Love Language

As I suggested earlier, you should get to know your job seeker's love languages. As a spouse, it is important to know and communicate yours as well.

Speaking of love, let us touch on physical intimacy. The experts say that job seekers, especially men, need more physical intimacy than ever to affirm your love, respect, and support. Add in extra touches, hugs, and hand-holding during the transition. [21-4]

How to Handle Finances during the Job Search

"Money is at the root of many marital issues.", as Lisa Bower stated in her article "Helping a Spouse Through Job Loss". [21-5] The foundation of security is shaken when finances are in question, adding extra stress to an already difficult situation.

Job seekers and their families need to prioritize and make adjustments in their spending while they are not bringing in as much income as before. Once a person enters the job transition, the spouse should sit down with the job seeker and develop a financial plan.

There are right and wrong ways to handle this. One female job seeker asked her husband if they could discuss their finances now that she was in a job search. Her husband towered over her as she sat at a table and challenged her to come up with any areas *he* needed to cut back on due to *her* situation. His body language and tone clearly communicated that she was on this ride alone; his life would not be impacted by this change. Another couple sat on the same side of the table with pencil and paper and worked together to decide how together they were going to make it through her transition. It may not surprise you to know that the first marriage did not work out; the second marriage survived the transition.

The job search will not take forever, but temporary cutbacks will relieve the financial pressures. Cut non-essential expenses and reduce other expenses immediately to give yourselves a cushion.

Areas to consider cutting:

- Television Programming: Whether cable or satellite, consider cutting back from higher level packages to basic programming or, if your situation allows, eliminate it altogether for now. There may be legitimate reasons not to disconnect cable services completely, though, especially if that is your major source of current events or is the spouse's escape once the job search tasks are done each day.

- Phone: If both spouses have cell phones, consider eliminating the home phone. There are other services available, such as magicJack, that offer free local and long distance service within the US and Canada, some require the use of a computer and some do not.

- Eating Out Budget: Consider cutting back on the number of times you eat out. Make the times you do eat out special.

- Look for ways to save: With the Internet, there are a growing number of ways to save on groceries, eating out, and attending events. It takes a little bit of work to find the best programs to tap into, but once you find them, they are easy to use. Use the link provided at the back of this book for up-to-date information and links to resources that will help you save.

- Clark Howard is a syndicated consumer advocate and my hero. I highly recommend his web site which contains important information about how to prioritize bills when the income does not meet the outflow. www.ClarkHoward.com.

- Reset priorities and set new goals.

That does not mean you have to put your life on hold. As Peter Bourke's book *A Better Way to Make a Living and a Life* suggests, consider quitting the race to keep up with the Joneses and consider living a simpler life, allowing you to live on less.

While making financial plans, determine what to do with any retirement funds such as a 401(k), and healthcare benefits.

Contact the credit card companies and ask for the hardship department. They may defer payments and interest for a number of months.

Work together to develop a financial plan for the transition and even beyond.

Involve the Entire Family

I do not have children, but I pay close attention to advice professionals give parents on how to handle kids when the family is going through any type of event (divorce, job loss, etc.). The advice is consistent: 21-6

1) Do not try to hide the event from the children. They will sense something is up and their imaginations will take them to the worst scenario. They may feel it is their fault.

2) The approach to use should be based on the age of the child.

3) Involve them in the solution. Just like you, they will be impacted by the job search and will feel better if they can do something to be involved in the solution. This may be a good time for everyone to look at decluttering and selling the things they no longer need or want.

4) As Donna Partow suggests in her article "Abiding Unemployment", do not answer their requests for "things" with "once we find a job". Instead, simply answer "yes" or "no". [21-7]

5) Have regular family meetings to discuss updates and then end the planning meeting with a fun activity.

6) Assure them this is a temporary situation, things will be okay, and keep them informed.

I remember back to Second Grade when my father retired from the Navy in Florida and was looking for a job in another state. We moved temporarily to North Carolina into my Grandfather's house, and I attended school with my cousin until Dad found his next job and a house for us.

My poor cousin! He not only had to take his girl cousin to school with him, but I cried nearly every day in class without apparent cause. I knew something was going on in our family's life, but I did not understand.

Children can get clingy, scared [21-8] (like me), or act out when they are responding to the changes in the family. Bring in examples of transitions in their short lives (like being promoted from one grade to the next or changing schools) to assure them this is just a temporary event. [21-9]

In the endnotes I reference some great articles to read on this topic.

When You Need Help and Advice or Think You Might

There may come a time when you both need help keeping the roof over your heads, food on the table, or the car in the driveway. As we already discussed in Step 1, there are organizations that exist to help.

Call 211 as soon as you realize you may need assistance or want to know what options are available. Do not wait until things are desperate; there are more options available for assistance the earlier in the process that you call.

Credit counseling, information on the latest mortgage programs, and couples counseling are all available for free or on a sliding scale through the 211 agencies.

If you feel that couples counseling will help, ask the job search spouse to go with you. Say you are asking them to do this for both of you. Be careful so that the focus is not on the job seeker; you do not want them to feel that you consider them broken. If the job seeking spouse will not go with you, go anyway so you can deal with your emotions and provide the positive environment the job seeker needs. If they do go, be sure to give them positive reinforcement for doing what you both needed. [21-10]

Impact on the Family Routine

The job search will have an impact on some of the family routines. [21-11] Keep to routines as much as possible but understand, expect, and plan for the impacts to the family schedule that will result with a spouse being out of employment. For instance, the job seekers may need access to the family computer more. If you were at home most days, having the spouse at home may throw off your routine. Understand these impacts, discuss them, and develop a plan that works.

While the job seeker is spending all hours searching for their next job, you may have an increase in your responsibilities. This may be because they are not available at times when they are needed or because you want to offload some of the pressure from them.

To handle this impact to the family schedule, you and your spouse may need to back out of time-consuming activities that are not as fulfilling. You want to keep from being overcommitted when you need extra time and energy for yourselves. In today's world, many of us have allowed ourselves to become overcommitted and other people have taken advantage of our "can do attitude". After all, there is the theory: "If you want something done, give it to the person who is already doing everything". You may be the person they are talking about. Now you need to take care of yourself and your family, so give others the opportunity to step up and assist with outside commitments.

Impact on Family Time

It is sometimes hard to understand why the job seeking spouse must be away in the evenings after going out so often during the day to meet people for coffee or lunch. It is important to realize and remember that the job search is a temporary situation and networking is an important step to getting a job.

Most networking events are held before or after work because the volunteers for the various networking groups have commitments during the day. This, however, takes away from your valuable family time. Understand it is necessary that your job seeker attend such events. Again, it is important to realize and remember that the job search is a temporary situation. Do not make negative comments or show negative body language when your spouse mentions a meeting or leaves for these events. You should, instead, encourage your spouse to get out and network and stay in touch with their contacts in the industry, including former coworkers.

Speaking of former coworkers, some job seekers tend to shut down and close off from former coworkers. Encourage them to stay in touch. At one company, the group of people who were impacted by a layoff created a group that met regularly at first while each member processed the loss. Not only did the group provide great emotional support, but they were a great source for industry networking as well.

If your job seeker is not willingly going out and meeting with others, get someone of the same gender that they trust to get them out of the house. [21-12] The friend may ask for the job seeker's help to work on a project the friend needs done. Once the project is done, the job seeker will have a renewed sense of success, accomplishment, and connection with the world.

Some job networking groups offer separate break-out groups for spouses. Sadly, there are not many groups that offer this feature. If you hear of one that does, you may want to check it out.

Offer to join your spouse at one of the job networking groups they regularly attend so you can see what the meetings are like.

Do not do anything that knowingly has a negative impact on your job seeker's chances. One mistake I saw a spouse make was to accompany the job seeker to a meeting with a young child in tow. The child was disruptive to the meeting for everyone. If the future hiring manager was in attendance, the job seeker blew a chance at getting employed. Some networking events offer child care, though most do not.

Realize there will probably be an impact on the family schedule, so plan for it and remember it is only temporary.

Communication

It is important to have open and honest communication. It is okay to say that you are afraid. Just be sure to add that you count on them and do not try to tell them how to conduct the job search. [21-13]

You want to keep the lines of communication open. Agree upon the when and what types of communication to have, but communicate!

This is the time you need to hold the tough conversations about relocation. Consider the real possibility that the next best opportunity may be in another town, and discuss whether or not that will work for the family. [21-14] Realize, though, that except for high level executive positions, many companies today do not offer relocation benefits.

One job seeker wanted to assure her husband that the job search was moving forward but without feeling she was having to "report in". She created a work plan (like a Microsoft Project Plan) and left it where her husband could see it so he could be assured of the progress that was being made.

Remember there is preparation work (Steps 1 – 3), a lot of marketing materials to create, and a lot of meetings to attend in order to find the job. It is a process and it takes time.

Wives: A good book to read is *Have a New Husband by Friday*. In addition to detailing action items to take to change the dynamic in the relationship, it states what most men want: to know that you respect, need, and want them; that you are their best friend; and they are the provider and they do it well.

This would also be a good time for both spouses to read the book *Men are from Mars, Women are from Venus* to understand how men and women communicate differently. For instance, men, when a woman asks you "Can you do <whatever>" we do not mean to challenge your capabilities. When a woman says that same thing to another woman, we mean it as, "Are you available and willing?" [21-15]

Men and women are different in many ways, and understanding these ways will help improve communication.

Taking Care of YOU

Something you hear every time you fly is a good analogy for life, "Put on your own oxygen mask before helping others". Taking care of yourself gives your spouse one less thing to worry about. [21-16]

You are affected by the job transition as much as your job seeking spouse. The family finances are limited, the daily schedule is impacted, and the emotions you and the job seeking spouse feel are real and different. You may be anxious for the future.

There are things you can do, some together, some separately, to be supportive of your spouse's job search. You need to do things to take care of you, too.

As the job seeker's partner, you need to feel loved as well. Now that you know what your love language is, negotiate for it. For instance, if your love language is quality time, then pick a night when there are no important networking meetings and create a date night. There are many special things you, as a couple, can do that do not cost a lot. Realize that during this transition, you may need to give more to your job seeking spouse than you receive. Once your spouse has landed a job, then it is your turn to be the receiver. Negotiate up front what you want so you have something to look forward to.

There is a Caregiver (Stress) Syndrome where the caregiver starts to have physical and emotional issues because they are so concerned with providing support to other people. It is a result of not taking care of themselves. [21-17]

During the time my mother was very ill with cancer, my sister started to experience Caregiver's Syndrome. I lived out of town so my sister needed to take care of my mother's immediate needs. She did not see alternatives to providing those needs. She was not leaving my mother's side and stress started to build. There were plenty of people who wanted to help, they just did not know how to. We identified little things they could do such as stopping by and sitting with our mother so my sister could have time for herself. A trip to the store felt like a treat. My sister needed times when she was taking care of herself, so she could have what it took to care for our mother. She had to put her own oxygen mask on first.

The something you do for yourself does not have to be expensive. While the spouse is out in the evening at important networking meetings, have a neighbor baby-sit the kids so you can get out of the house or if you are like me, have the house to yourself, maybe enjoying a luxurious bubble bath.

Do not give your "honey do" lists to the job seeker believing they have unlimited time to work on the items while they are not working. Those chores will take the focus and time away from their job search efforts. They may even offer to do these tasks because they get the immediate sense of satisfaction of a job well done or are relieved to put off a job search step they find less comfortable (like networking). All that these chores will do is elongate the job search.

Have an emotional outlet, a trusted someone of the same gender, to talk to. You do not want to place extra anxiety on your spouse so find someone who is not a close family member or does not have a relationship with your spouse. Make sure the person you confide in knows how to a keep confidence and is positive by nature. Do not let anyone pull you down during this time.

If you wake up at night with your thoughts spinning, get up, write down what you are thinking and then get back to bed.

Be sure to put on your own oxygen mask first so you are able to help others.

Have Fun

The entire family can feel they are walking on eggshells during the job transition. Release that stress with fun. [21-18]

Watch funny movies together; get outside when the weather is nice; tell jokes or remember your most embarrassing moments and share them.

If the spouse is not feeling great about their physical shape, consider activities that are fun and burn calories, making sure not to take away the "fun" aspect. As the job seeker becomes physically active, it will restore a sense of accomplishment and control. The more their self-confidence builds, the better chance they have of landing the job.

Type into your favorite search engine the words "free events" and the name of your town. It may take a little research and some creativity but have fun. Laughter is a great stress reliever so find ways to bring laughter into the family dynamics.

Have a Date Night Each Week

Speaking of fun, have a date night each week. [21-19] Date nights do not have to be expensive; there are many free things you can do. The most important aspect of date night is that the job search goes completely on hold, and the time is spent enjoying and appreciating each other. You can be creative with what you do, or routine activities may be more comforting, depending on which you both prefer.

Set aside time for the two of you to have fun.

How <u>Not</u> to Help: Assist but Do Not Take Over

Your job during this transition is to provide a consistent positive environment and to be your spouse's biggest cheerleader.

I have seen spouses take over the job search. In more than one instance, the spouse took the job seeker to a networking meeting and did all of the work for the job seeker. They asked all of the questions, gathered all of the handouts, and did all of the talking. This does not build the job seeker's self-confidence.

Life Coach Syble Solomon reminds women, "becoming the chief breadwinner has been empowering, but many women are suffering because their husbands are suffering from a lack of self-esteem [tied to their job loss]. They are doing everything they can to minimize and play down the fact that they are the primary breadwinner."[21-20] Be careful with your words if you offer to go to work or find additional work. Your husband may hear this as "you are not an adequate provider".

Helping your spouse with the job search is a good thing to do, just be sure it enhances their chances. At a meeting where I was the guest speaker, a job seeker handed me her networking card, and I noticed it was printed crooked. I asked if she knew about a company that provides professional networking cards for free (other than the price of shipping). She said she knew of such companies, but her husband wanted to help her job search and created the cards for her. Having unprofessional cards does not help.

You can offer to assist your spouse with their job search, just do not take over or do anything that hurts their chances. The important role you have is to be your job seeker's safe harbor.

In the Voice of Job Seekers

The following are the best and worst things job seekers said a spouse did for them.

Worst: Keeping the candidate from getting to their

appointment on time.

– Deb H.

My wife suggested [to] me the book " What Color is Your

Parachute". It is a comprehensive guide on job search which

everyone involved in job search must read.

- Jai M.

My wife ALWAYS remained positive and supportive by

reminding me how the Lord will ALWAYS take care of us.

– Gil J.

My wife pretty much has left me to do it and encouraged me

when I needed it. She has stood by anxiously but supported

me all the way.

– Steve C.

My wife continued to believe in me. She does not know

exactly what I do for a living, but she supported my every move. I married my best friend and she is still my best friend.

– Jim B.

Patience is the absolute best thing a spouse can [have] during this time. If the patience runs out, you will end up taking just any job out there and quite possibly ruin any hopes of a decent career. Pressure is the worst thing that a job seeker can face. The normal pressure can be extreme without anyone else adding to it.

- Doug N.

My spouse asking about my day, just as she did when I was working, is [the] most important [thing] to me and adding her positive reinforcement to my accomplishments for the day. Both of which she does well.

– Dave W.

The best thing that my spouse did was have me to specifically write down what I was going to do on a daily basis. Make sure I leave the house at a certain time, as if I was actually working, to get me acclimated as if I was working.

– Mary T.

My wife usually sends me a text (Good luck, I love you) just before an interview. She's been most supportive during this time.

– Steve B.

[From a recruiter:] Worst: Answering the phone like an idiot. Demanding to know from a female recruiter why she's calling their husband, asking the caller to call back after they've turned on voice mail, telling the caller that the person looking wouldn't be interested in their job, hanging up on the caller, not giving messages to the candidate. And, yes...I've had all of these things happen to me more times than I care to recount. And I'm not just referring to when I'm cold calling candidates -- I'm referring to times when I've been working with candidates who really wanted a job I

had to offer and were already in process. Oh, yeah...and by

the way, people have done these very same things to hiring

managers. Ouch!

- Deb H.

My wife was understanding, encouraging, and supportive

(within reason). We had several discussions at various times

during my unemployment related to:

* Our family financial situation

* My current / future job prospects in my job search

* My attitude toward taking a lesser position / lower salary

than my previous positions

* God's faithfulness to provide for our needs

She seemed intuitively to sense the right response at the

right time to keep me moving forward in my job search.

Sometimes she kicked my butt to keep me in the game. Other

times she offered encouraging words when I was

disillusioned and discouraged.

In addition, she never spoke negatively about me with our

children. She recognized the difficulty facing a man in his fifties during a job search given the changing corporate

culture and current economic conditions.

I can't imagine that my wife could have, or should have,

done anything differently to support me during my job

search.

- Mike M.

From a previous job seeker: A friend of mine sent me their

husband's résumé saying that it would be a rough

Christmas for their kids unless he found a job soon. I read it

and forwarded it to a business associate that I felt was a

match. He got the job! Their gratitude humbled me.

NEVER underestimate the power of networking.

- Luis C.

Best thing - my wife was unbelievably supportive of me.

– Peter W.

The best thing my spouse does for me is to give the support I

need as I continue my search. I work very hard finding that next great career and my wife acts as my angel in providing

the financial (she has a job), emotional and partnership

support during these very difficult times. I am an extremely

positive, passionate, and upbeat individual but always helps

to get the boost you need to continue in that frame of mind.

- Al F.

Worst thing- I was married several years ago the first time I

got downsized. I was sitting on the couch crying when my

wife walked in and sat down. I told her what happened, and

after several profanities, etc., she asked "Now what are we

going to do you stupid....(fill in the blank)?" That hurt more

than anything ever. The last thing someone needs at a time

like that is to experience verbal and mental abuse. Those

hurts last many, many years.

- Greg H.

At one time, I was in a company and position where I was

miserable. I didn't feel I was receiving any guidance or

leadership from my supervisor, and I felt like I was going

nowhere. I was conflicted, because there were aspects of the job itself that I enjoyed, but the environment was somewhat toxic and I was mired in a "victim" mentality. As I was looking for another job, my fiancé helped me keep my feet on the ground - he helped me determine what I was really looking for, and weigh the pros and cons of different options. Ultimately, I was offered a position in another organization and chose not to take it, because when I was able to look at it objectively, it wasn't a good fit for me. I decided to stay where I was and make the best of my situation. Shortly thereafter, I received a promotion that moved me into a different department, with a different supervisor and more long-term options. Removing the emotional reactions and focusing on objective measures was the best thing I could have done, and he definitely pointed me in that direction.
– Anonymous

I know that the hardest thing to handle (for this man, anyway) is failing as a provider, not being able to find a way to take care of my family. My wife's absolute belief that she had chosen well boxed me into first acting like I thought so too. Eventually, either from lying to myself loudly and long or from the belief that I had also chosen well, I came around to what she obviously knew to be true -- she could never have chosen a mate who could not take care of her. Pride took over then. I will never stop wanting her to be proud of me.

– Robert P.

My wife moved 1,000 miles for a job I knew I would succeed at. Ultimately, it has led to a higher standard of living for the both of us, but she willingly relocated to a state she had never set foot in so that I could be happy with my employment.

- Daniel K.

Chapter Summary

When one spouse is unemployed, the family is unemployed. Take the job search one day at a time. There will be good days and bad days.

Both spouses need to process the loss and then develop a plan to handle finances and changes in the family schedule. Be your job seeker's biggest cheerleader and offer consistent support.

Do not cut yourself off from others, this is when you need them the most and other people want to help; let them know how they can.

Take care of yourself. Keep the lines of communication open and draw closer together as you go through this temporary challenge. Remember to build in fun.

Believer's Bonus

Pray constantly, not out of desperation but knowing that God has a plan and is in control. Count your blessings. If you look at the news, you will see so many others who have nothing, and some of them do not have the love of God in their lives.

"Because he loves me," says the Lord, "I will rescue him; I will protect him for he acknowledges my name. He will call upon me, and I will answer him; I will be with him in trouble, I will deliver him and honor him."

- *Psalm 91:14-15*

He who finds a wife finds what is good and receives favor from the Lord.

- *Proverbs 18:22*

Better to live on a corner of the roof than share a house with a quarrelsome wife. Better to live in a desert than with a quarrelsome and ill-tempered wife.

- *Proverbs 21:9,19*

A wife of noble character who can find? She is worth far more than rubies. Her husband has full confidence in her and lacks nothing of value.

- *Proverbs 31:10-11*

"Do not store up for yourselves treasures on earth, where moth and rust destroy, and where thieves break in and steal. But store up for yourselves treasures in heaven, where moth and rust do not destroy, and where thieves do not break in and steal. For where your treasure is, there your heart will be also. ...No one can serve two masters."

- *Matthew 6:19-21, 24*

"I have come that they may have life, and have it to the full".

- *John 10:10*

Do not be anxious about anything, but in everything, by prayer and petition, with thanksgiving, present your request to God. And the peace of God, which transcends all understanding, will guard

your hearts and your minds in Christ Jesus.

- *Philippians 4:6-7*

And my God will meet all your needs according to his glorious

riches in Christ Jesus.

- *Philippians 4:19*

Be joyful always; pray continually; give thanks in all

circumstances, for this is God's will for you in Christ Jesus.

- *1 Thessalonians 5:16-18*

There is no fear in love. But perfect love drives out fear.

- *1 John 4:18*

"My grace is sufficient for you, for my power is made perfect in

weakness." Therefore I will boast all the more gladly about my

weakness so that Christ's power may rest on me.

– *2 Corinthians 12:9*

Chapter 22

What to do When Your Job Seeker

Seems Stuck or has Given Up

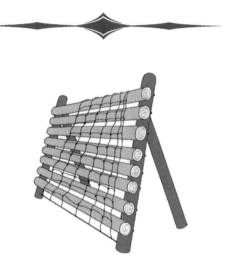

22.1 The Obstacle – Easier to Overcome with the Net(work)

It takes longer to find a job during this recession than it

did when the economy was booming. It is important that you do

not mistake the duration of the search as an indication that the job seeker is stuck. The job seeker is stuck if there is no forward progress and they have run out of ideas and motivation.

When a job seeker has been in a job search for more than a year, though, it may be for one of the following three reasons:

1) The job seeker has not chosen a positive attitude. The job seeker may not have had a good attitude initially before starting the search. Job seekers must give themselves permission and time to go through the grieving process, get to the point of acceptance, and even get excited about the opportunities that lie ahead.

    The job seeker may have started with a good attitude, but if they are not making progress because they are not conducting the search the right way, or if there is an unsupportive environment, it will be hard, if not impossible, to maintain a good attitude.

Add to a bad attitude the silence when applying for positions, rejection when they are not selected, the unknown, the feeling of not being good enough and not providing, and the job seeker may experience an attitude of hopelessness.

2) The job seeker has not taken an inventory of their skills, abilities, and accomplishments and learned to articulate their competitive advantage.

As we have already discussed, you would not think about selling a product without knowing the product, how it works, and why it is better than your competition's. Job seekers cannot sell themselves without knowing how a company will benefit by hiring them. When job seekers do not know their competitive advantages and how to articulate them, it means the marketing materials (including the résumé), the efforts to network, and the interview will fail.

3) The majority of job seekers are using the wrong approach in searching for the job. As stated in Chapter 7 - Search, networking is the best approach for finding the job lead and getting the interview.

Instead, too many job seekers solely rely on applying online for jobs or tapping into the limited network they had before they lost their job. Not only is that approach unproductive, it causes the job seeker to spend too much time at home, increasing the isolation they feel. By staying at home, the job seeker does not get the sunshine (Vitamin D) they need to stay positive [22-1], and the lack of response from the applications only causes further depression. After a while, the job seeker will become immobilized by this depression.

We have already said you cannot do the search for them without destroying their self-confidence even further. "Depression...can trap a person in their own prison", as Erika Krull states in her article "When a Depresses Spouse Refuses Help". [22-2] They do not want to be there but are not able to "shake it off" or "pull themselves up by their boot straps". Then they start to feel worse about themselves. Something has to break this unending cycle. If the job seeker has clinical depression, professional help may be needed. [22-3]

If they do not have clinical depression, there are a few things you can do to help get them unstuck.

1) Tell them it is not them; tell them you just discovered how much the job market has changed. Assure them that by knowing how it changed and doing what the new job market requires, they will get the job and that you are there to help.

2) If the attitude is more from the lack of results, it would be wise to call in another type of professional – a job search

coach. No one would enter a championship round of a sporting event without the right equipment, without a coach for instruction or feedback, and without practicing. Yet many people go into a job search, where a livelihood is on the line, without the right equipment (a list of prior accomplishments and powerful marketing materials) and without practicing (interviews). Even if you have the training, do not try to coach your loved one; you are too close to the situation. You may consider offering to hire a job search coach to give them that expert assistance and, if they prefer, they can arrange to pay you back once they are employed.

3) The best thing you can do is give your job seeker your consistent positive support during the job transition using the principles outlined in this guide. Consistency is the key. You cannot be hard on them one moment and supportive the next.

4) The job seeker may want to consider a temporary job in their field. Working as a temporary worker (in their field) will increase and maintain core skills, and it is a great way to network into a permanent job. Companies like this approach, which I refer to as "trying before buying".

5) Get your job seeker out of the house and involved in fun physical activities. [22-4] By getting sun, they will increase their Vitamin D, which improves mood [22-2], and the physical activity will increase the positive hormones.

You cannot change another person and motivation comes from within. You can only do what you can to provide them the right environment and support to succeed. By implementing what you have learned in *Found a Job Yet?*, you have started in that direction.

Chapter Summary

Motivation has to come from within the job seeker. Your job is to provide a consistent supportive environment.

Believer's Bonus

When the job search has taken a long time without results, you start to wonder if you missed a turn; that God wanted you to take a turn that you did not. I know from experience that, like the signs along the side of the interstate, you will receive a periodic sign to let you know if you are on the right road. Just ask God and listen for His quiet voice.

But I trust in you, O Lord; I say "You are my God". My times are in your hands.

- Psalm 31:14

We wait in hope for the Lord; he is our help and our shield.

- Psalm 33:20-21

Delight yourself in the Lord and he will give you the desires of your heart. Commit your way to the Lord; trust in him and he will do this: He will make your righteousness shine like the dawn, the justice of your cause like the noonday sun. Be still before the Lord and wait patiently for him.

- *Psalm 37: 4-7*

Be still, and know that I am God.

- *Psalm 46:10*

He gives strength to the weary and increases the power of the weak. Even youths grow tired and weary, and young men stumble and fall; but those who hope in the Lord will renew their strength. They will soar on wings like eagles; they will run and not grow weary, they will walk and not be faint.

- *Isaiah 40:29-31*

Consider him who endured such opposition from sinful men, so that you will not grow weary and lose heart.

- *Hebrews 12:3*

Consider it pure joy my brothers, whenever you face trial of many kinds, because you know that the testing of your faith develops perseverance. Perseverance must finish its work so that you may be mature and complete, not lacking anything. If any of you lacks wisdom, he should ask God, who gives generously to all without finding fault, and it will be given to him. But when he asks, he must believe and not doubt.

- *James 1:2-6*

Appendices

Appendix A - Ask Others Form

Please consider these categories and questions to provide feedback I will factor in selecting my next position and company.

ACCOMPLISHMENTS
What are the top things I should remember that I have accomplished?

ABILITIES
What am I best at? What 3 or 4 abilities should be at the core of what I do every day?

INTERESTS
Where do you feel I most readily invest time, energy, talent, and money? What do I seem to enjoy most?

PERSONALITY
What positive personality traits come to mind when you think of me?

VALUES
What positive values and character strengths do I have?

UNIQUE
What am I known for? What comes easily to me?

"PERFECT" CAREER FIT
If there were no restrictions, what do you think would be the perfect career fit for me?

Appendix B - Networking Guide Template

Joy C. Kerr

3700 Mansell Road
Alpharetta, Georgia 30022

(770) 555-1212
JoyCKerr@email.com

http://www.linkedin.com/in/joyckerr

CHANGE/PROCESS MANAGEMENT

Extensive experience in change management, process management, and project management. Additional experience in coordinating and implementing systems and processes for records administration, operational processes, instrument calibration and repair, and customer service.

EXTENSIVE EXPERIENCE

Change Management	Process Management	Project Management
• Integrated QA processes • Revised procedures and training due to new management principles	• Re-engineered • Instituted new computer system to increase efficiency in laboratory process	• Implemented new software and hardware systems for laboratory

TARGET MARKET/TARGET COMPANIES

Desired Geographic Areas:
    Atlanta based company or 70%+ time spent in Atlanta w/ some travel opportunities

Industries: Energy, Utilities, Electronics, Manufacturing, Consulting, and Process/Change Management

Titles: Manager, Director, Project Manager, Change Management

Energy/Nuclear/Power	Electronics	Manufacturing/Other
INPO	Siemens Power	UPS
Siemens Power	Scientific Atlanta	Lockheed Martin
MEAG		Kimberly Clark

Appendix C - Additional Resources

Here are a few of the additional resources you and your

job seeker may find helpful.

Go to www.FoundaJobYet.com/Updates for an updated

list of additional books on this topic.

REALITY OF THE NEW JOB MARKET

A Better Way to Make a Living and a Life by Peter Bourke
www.betterwaytomakealiving.com

STEP 1 – ATTITUDE

Who Moved My Cheese by Spencer Johnson

Attitude is Everything – 10 Life Changing Steps to Turning Attitude Into Action by Keith Harrell

The Power of Positive Thinking by Norman Vincent Peale

The Bible especially Psalm and Proverbs

STEP 2 – APTITUDE

StrengthsFinder 2.0 by Tom Rath
(includes an online assessment)

What Color is Your Parachute? by Richard Bolles

The Five Languages of Appreciation in the Workplace
by Gary Chapman and Paul White

STEP 3 – ALTITUDE

The Biz Journal for most major cities.

> Go to www.bizjournal.com to get the name of the business journal for your area. For Atlanta, the Biz Journal is the *Atlanta Business Chronicle*.

Other business news outlets (example: Crain's for Chicago)

Book of Lists by the area biz journals.

MARKETING MATERIALS

Resume Magic By Susan Whitcomb

Find a Job Through Social Networking by Diane Crompton and Ellen Sautter

Cover Letter: *"The Most Powerful Cover Letter"* by Judi Adams at RightChangesJobSearchCoach.blogspot.com

Networking Guide: *"What Document is as Valuable to a Job Seeker as a Great Résumé"* by Judi Adams at RightChangesJobSearchCoach.blogspot.com

Knock'em Dead Cover Letters by Martin Yate

Me 2.0 by Dan Schawbel

STEP 4 – SEARCH

How to Get Your Point Across in 30 Seconds or Less
by Milo O. Frank

How to Work a Room – Your Essential Guide to Savvy Socializing
by Susan RoAne

Face to Face: How to Reclaim the Personal Touch in a Digital World by Susan RoAne

The Art of Mingling by Jeanne Martinet

The Definitive Book of Body Language
by Allan and Barbara Pease

Dig Your Well Before You're Thirsty by Harvey Mackay

The Networking Survival Guide by Diane Darling

STEP 5 – SORT

101 Dynamite Questions to Ask at Your Job Interview
by Richard Fein

Interview Magic by Susan Whitcomb

The Definitive Book of Body Language
by Allan and Barbara Pease

Sixty Seconds & You're Hired by Robin Ryan

STEP 6 – SELECT

Bible

RELATIONSHIPS

Men are From Mars, Women are From Venus,
   by John Gray PhD.

Have a New Husband by Friday, by Dr. Kevin Leman

The Art of Helping by Lauren Littauer Briggs

The Five Love Languages: The Secret to Love That Lasts, ©2010
   by Gary Chapman (Northfield Publishing)

The Five Languages of Appreciation in the Workplace
   by Gary Chapman and Paul White

How to Really Love Your Adult Child
   by Ross Campbell and Gary Chapman

Effective Listening Skills by Dennis Kratz
   and Abby Robinson

The Seven Bridges, Marriage: A Journey Designed by God,
   www.sevenbridgemarriage.com

Appendix D- *Using the Crossroads Career® Materials*

Crossroads/Career
Network

You know how bad the unemployment situation is today.
Imagine being in a search without a resource to go to so you can learn
the latest job search techniques. What is worse, imagine being in a
search without the assurance and peace from God. CCN will serve as a
tremendous resource for your school, church community outreach
program, or coaching practice. It provides an incredible opportunity to
introduce or help strengthen someone's personal relationship with
Jesus Christ.

Your annual membership to Crossroads Career® Network
gives you full access to the website and a wealth of Christian career
resources focused on job search, career development, and career
information. You will be a part of and have access to the network of
other schools, churches, and coaches in the world who are members of
the Crossroads family. For more information, go to:

www.FoundaJobYet.com/CrossroadsCareerServices

Appendix E - Legend of Illustrations

Appendix F - Link to Updates

Change is happening faster than ever before. In order to provide the most current and relevant information, a website with updates to *Found a Job Yet?* has been provided.

Update Link

For the latest information go to

www.FoundaJobYet.com/Updates

Comments and Proposed Updates

If you would like to send a comment to Judi Adams about *Found a Job Yet?* or would like to propose an update, send an e-mail to **Updates@FoundaJobYet.com**.

Appendix G - Order Additional Copies

Individual Copies

To order additional individual copies of *Found a Job Yet?* go to **www.FoundaJobYet.com/Order**.

Group Orders

For group orders of 50 or more, send an e-mail to **Group@FoundaJobYet.com**.

Appendix H - End Notes

1-1 Linda Levine, Domestic Social Policy Division, *Congressional Research Service Report (RL31250), The Worker Adjustment and Retraining Notification Act Warn*, http://assets.opencrs.com/rpts/RL31250_20080109.pdf, (Jan. 2008)

1-2 David Glenn, *Buy American an Interview with Dana Frank Issue #19*, *www.stayfreemagazine.org/archives/19/danafrank.html*

1-3 Charles Erwin Wilson, President of General Motors, Report to a Senate Armed Services Committee, Confirmation Hearings, 1952

1-4 Linda Levine, *"Unemployment Through Layoffs: What Are the Underlying Reasons?"*, Federal Publications, http://digitalcommons.ilr.cornell.edu/cgi/viewcontent.cgi?article=1190 &context=key_workplace, (2005)

1-5 Michael King, *Atlanta City Council Approves Revised Pension Plan*, http:www.11alive.com/news/article/196256/40/Atlanta_City_Council _Approves_Revised_Pension_Plan, (June 2011)

   Reuters, *Lockheed union workers approve labor pact*, http://www.reuters.com/article/2011/03/07/us-lockheed-idUSTRE7260NI20110307, (Mar 2011)

1-6 Laura Petrecca, USA Today, More Companies Cut or End 401(k) Plan Matches, http://www.usatoday.com/money/perfi/retirement/2009-03-25-company-match-retirement_N.htm, (March 2009)

1-7 Diane Stafford, ABWA Management, *The New Workforce Just In Time Delivery*, (2011)

   Beth Cooper, *Employee Trends The On-Demand* Workforce, http://sixsigmaresource.blogspot.com/2010/04/employee-trends-on-demand-workforce-by.html, (Apr 2010)

   Wikipedia, *Contingent Workforce*, http://en.wikipedia.org/wiki/Contingent_workforce

1-8 Dan Schawbel, *Top 10 Social Sites for Finding a Job*, http://mashable.com/2009/02/24/top-10-social-sites-for-finding-a-job, (Feb. 2009)

1-9 *Dot-Com Bubble Timeline*, http://timelines.com/topics/dot-com-bubble

Market Crashes: Housing Bubble and Credit Crisis (2007-2009), http://www.investopedia.com/features/crashes/crashes9.asp#axzz1b YXjjz18

Erin McCune, *Lessons for Bankers from the Telecom Bust (The Economist)*, http://paymentsviews.com/2009/03/01/lessons-for-bankers-from-the-telecom-bust-the-economist/, (Mar 2009)

1-10 *Economist's View: What Jobs are Safe from Offshoring?*, http://economistsview.typepad.com/economistsview/2006/03/what_j obs_are_s.html, (Mar 2006)

Offshoring, http://en.wikipedia.org/wiki/Offshoring

1-11 Atlanta Business Chronicle, *FDIC: Bank Failures in Brief 2011*, www.fdic.gov/bank/historical/bank

Wallace Witkowski, *Georgia Bank Failures Bring 2011 US Tally to 42*, http://www.marketwatch.com/story/georgia-bank-failures-bring-2011-us-tally-to-42-2011-05-20, (May 2011)

1-12 Carl Bonham, Department of Economics, University of Hawaii at Manoa, and Christopher Edmonds, Department of Economics, University of Hawaii at Manoa and Research Department, East-West Center, *The Impact of 9/11 and Other Terrible Global Events on Tourism in the U.S. and Hawaii, Working Paper No. 06-2*, http://www.economics.hawaii.edu/research/workingpapers/WP_06-2.pdf, (Jan 2006)

Arlene Fleming, *The After Effect for Air Travel Post 9/11*, http://airtravel.about.com/b/2006/09/10/the-after-effects-for-air-travel-post-911.htm, (Sep. 2006)

Economic Effects Arising From the September 11 Attacks, http://en.wikipedia.org/wiki/Economic_effects_arising_from_the_Sept ember_11_attacks

1-13 Rick Wartzman, *Behind America's 'Jobless Recovery'*,
http://www.businessweek.com/management/behind-americas-
jobless-recovery-07152011.html

1-14 Peter Valdes-Dapena, CNN Money, *Japan Earthquake Impact Hits U.S.
Auto Plants*,
http://money.cnn.com/2011/03/28/autos/japan_earthquake_autos_ou
tlook/index.htm, (Mar. 2011)

1-15 *Louisiana Oil Spill 2010 Photos: Gulf of Mexico Disaster Unfolds*,
http://www.huffingtonpost.com/2010/04/30/louisiana-oil-spill-
2010_n_558287.html, (Sep. 2010)

1-16 Emma Clark, *SARS Strikes Down Asia Tourism*,
http://news.bbc.co.uk/2/hi/business/3024015.stm, (May 2003)

World Travel & Tourism Council, *SARS has a Massive Impact on Travel
and Tourism in Affected Destinations*,
http://www.wttc.org/eng/Tourism_News/Press_Releases/Press_Rele
ases_2003/Impact_of_SARS/

PKF Consulting, *The Impacts of the Iraq War & SARS on Canada's
Accommodations Industry Qtr 3 2003 Results*,
http://www.mtc.gov.on.ca/en/research/impact_studies/pkf_executiv
e_summaryq3_e.pdf (Dec 2003)

Department of Applied Economics, National Chung-Hsing University,
Taichung, Taiwan, *Assessing Impacts of SARS and Avian Flu on
International Tourism Demand to Asia Accepted Oct 31, 2007*, http://tugas-
pbw.comuf.com/penyakittropis/upload/B1.pdf, (Oct 2007)

1-17 Kelly Yamanouchi, Atlanta Journal Constitution, *Delta Trims Losses,
AirTran Posts Profit*, http://www.ajc.com/business/delta-trims-lossess-
aitran-97620.html, (Jul 2009)

1-18 Catherine Rampell, NY Times, *Average Length of Unemployment All-Time
High*, http://economix.blogs.nytimes.com/2011/06/03/average-length-
of-unemployment-at-all-time, (Jun 2011)

Table A-12 Unemployed Persons by Duration of Unemployment,
http://www.bls.gov/news.release/empsit.t12.htm

Sara E. Rix, AARP Public Policy Institute, *The Unemployment Situation, April 2011: Average Duration of Unemployment for Older Jobseekers Exceeds One Year*, http://www.aarp.org/work/job-hunting/info-05-2011/fs225-employment.html, (May 2011)

1-19 Bureau of Labor Statistics, *How the Government Measures Unemployment*, http://www.bls.gov/cps/cps_htgm.htm

1-20 *Unemployment Benefits (by Country)*, http://en.wikipedia.org/wiki/unemployment_benefits

U.S. Department of Labor, *State Unemployment Insurance Benefits*, http://workforcesecurity.doleta.gov/unemploy/uifactsheet.asp

1-21 Bureau of Labor Statistics, *Table A-15. Alternative Measures of Labor Underutilization*, http://www.bls.gov/news.release/empsit.t15.htm

1-22 Annette Richmond, *Unhappy at Work? Lots of People Are*, http://www.career-intelligence.com/management/unhappy.asp

Lisa Johnson Mandell, *Most Business Professionals Are Unhappily Employed*, http://jobs.aol.com/articles/2011/03/04/most-business-professionals-are-unhappily-employed/,(Mar 2011)

1-23 US News, *Most Baby Boomers Plan to Delay Retirement*, http://money.usnews.com/money/blogs/planning-to-retire/2010/06/30/most-baby-boomers-plan-to-delay-retirement, (Jun 2010)

Baby Boomers: Delaying Retirement Becomes the New Tradition, http://www.theretirementreality.com/2011/09/09/baby-boomers-delaying-retirement-becomes-the-new-tradition/, (Sep 2011)

1-24 Bureau of Labor Statistics, *Repeated Spells of Unemployment National Longitudinal Surveys*, http://www.bls.gov/nls/nlsfaqs.htm

1-25 Bureau of Labor Statistics, *Job Openings and Labor Turnover (JOLT) Survey News Release*, http://www.bls.gov/news.release/jolts.htm

3-1 Elisabeth Kübler -Ross, David Kessler, *The Five Stages of Grief*, http://grief.com/the-five-stages-of-grief

3-2 *9-1-1*, Wikipedia.org/wiki/9-1-1

3-3 *4-1-1*, en.wikipedia.org/wiki/4-1-1

3-4 U.S. Department of Transportation, Federal Highway Administration, *511 Deployment*, http://www.fhwa.dot.gov/trafficinfo/511.htm

Transportation Canada, *511 Readiness in Canada*, www.tc.gc.ca/eng/innovation/tdc-projects-its-d-its06-1125.htm

3-5 Federal Communications Commission, *Dial 211 for Essential Community Services*, http://www.fcc.gov/guides/dial-211-essential-community-services

211Canada,ca, *211 for All Canada: Frequently Asked Questions*, www.211canada.ca/what.php

3-6 U.S. Department of Labor, *State Unemployment Insurance Benefits*, http://workforcesecurity.doleta.gov/unemploy/uifactsheet.asp

5-1 Joe Santana, *Hire Talent and Passion Over Skills & Experience*, http://www.zdnet.co.uk/news/systems-management/2002/11/12/hire-talent-and-passion-over-skill-and-experience-2125761/, (Nov 2002)

Employee Engagement, http://en.wikipedia.org/wiki/Employee_engagement

Hiring Trends: Down with the Degree, Up with the Passion, http://betterwaytomakealiving.com_wordpress/?p=690, (Feb 2011)

6-1 Malcolm Fleschner, *Resume Review: How to Find Qualified Candidates*, http://hiring.monster.com/hr/hr-best-practices/recruiting-hiring-advice/attracting-job-candidates/resume-review.aspx,

Donna Kehl, Online e-Recruiting Benefits & Challenges, http://www.talentflow.com/blogs/online-e-recruiting-benefits-and-challenges/,(Mar 2011)

Ann Machando, Creative Staffing, *Unqualified Job Applicants Distract & Prolong the Hiring Process!*, http://florida.jobing.com/blog_post.asp?post=19607,(Jun 2009)

Gareth Jones, www.linkedin.com/answers/career-education/job-search/CAR_JOB/545006-206308, (Sep 2009)

Larry Slesinger, *Why Qualified Candidates Don't Always Get the Best Jobs*, http://www.execsearches.com/articles/Why_Qualified_Candidates.htm, (Oct 2000)

Tim Tyrell-Smith, *Not Qualified For a Job? Don't Apply*, http://timsstrategy.com/quick-tip-unqualified-for-a-job-dont-apply

6-2 *Understanding What Employers Want in a Cover Letter*, www.dummies.com/how-to/content/understanding-what-employers-want-in-a-cover-lette.html

Anthony Balderrama, *Do You Still Need a Cover Letter?*, http://msn.careerbuilder.com/Article/MSN-1811-Cover-Letters-Resumes-Do-You-Still-Need-a-Cover-Letter/, (Feb 2009)

Robyn Ryan, *Dos and Don'ts of a Good Cover Letter*, http://msn.careerbuilder.com/Article/MSN-1300-Cover-Letters-Resumes-Dos-and-Donts-of-a-Good-Cover-Letter/, (Feb 2008)

6-3 Barbara Kiviat, *Why are Large Companies Losing More Jobs Than Smaller Ones*, http://www.time.com/time/business/article/0,8599,1882300,00.html (Feb 2009)

Paul Kedrosky, *Here's the Real Reason Small Companies Create All of the New Jobs*, http://articles.businessinsider.com/2010-04-09/markets/30034135_1_job-creation-wall-new-jobs, (Mar 2009)

Statistics About Business Size (Including Small Business) from the U.S. Census Bureau: Employment Size of Firms, http://www.census.gov/econ/smallbus.html

7-1 Right Management, *People Still Land Most Jobs Person to Person*, http://www.right.com/news-and-events/press-releases/2011-press-releases/item21493.aspx, (Jun 2011)

7-2 Martin Lieberman, *Uncovering the Hidden Job Market*, http://www.experience.com/alumnus/article?channel_id=career_man agement&source_page=jobs&article_id=article_1126286323915

Dr. Randall S. Hansen, *The Truth Behind the Hidden Job Market Myth*, http://www.quintcareers.com/Hidden_job_Market_release.html, (Jun 2010)

Hidden Job Market, http://www.jobbait.com/a/hidden_job_market.htm

Rachel Vilsack, Regional Labor Market Analyst & MN Department of Employment & Economic Development, *Uncover the Hidden Job Market*, http://rachelvilsack.com/wp-content/uploads/2011/05/LMI_Goodwill_May23.pdf, (May 2011

Derek Dostal, *Successful Job Search Marketing*, http://youstartmonday.com/successful-job-search-marketing/, (Jan 2011)

9-1 Matt McMillen, Health.com, *For Mental Health, Bad Job Worse Than No Job*, http://www.cnn.com/2011/HEALTH/03/14/unemployment.health/index.html, (Mar 2011)

Hans Villarica, *Study: Having a Bad Job is Worse than No Job For Mental Health*, http://healthland.time.com/2011/03/15/study-having-a-bad-job-is-worse-than-no-job-for-mental-health/, (Mar 2011)

Derek Thompson, Worse Than Unemployed? A Bad Job, http://www.theatlantic.com/business/archive/2011/03/worse-than-unemployment-a-bad-job/72547/, (Mar 2011)

R.M. Fox, Making the Right Decision the First Time: Avoid Taking the Wrong Job, http://toplinestrategies.com/humancapital/?p=1397

10-1 Jim Collins, HSM World Business Forum, Radio City Music Hall, Lunch with Speakers, (Sep 2008)

13-1 Rich Morin, Rakesh Kochhar, Lost Income, Lost Friends – and Loss of Self Respect: The Impact of Long-Term Unemployment, http://pewsocialtrends.org/files/2010/11/760-recession.pdf , (Jul 2010)

Focus on the Family Customer Help, *I'm suddenly unemployed; how do I tell my wife? What can I do to protect my family while I look for another job?*, http://family.custhelp.com/app/answers/detail/a_id/25752/~/i'm-suddenly-unemployed%3B-how-do-i-tell-my-wife%3F-what-can-i-do-to-protect-my, (Sep 2011)

Janet Wendy Spiegel response to post, *My Husband Lost His Job*, http://beingfrugal.net/2008/03/27/surviving-job-loss/ (Mar 2008)

Debra Bacon, *Supporting Your Spouse Through Job Loss*, http://www.theravive.com/blog/post/2010/02/22/Supporting-your-spouse-through-job-loss.aspx, (Feb 2010)

14-1 Chris Isidore, *The Great Recession*, http://money.cnn.com/2009/03/25/news/economy/depression_comparisons/, (Mar 2009)

14-2 Pew Research Center, *How to Comfort a Friend that has Lost a Corporate Job*, http://pewsocialtrends.org/files/2010/11/760-recession.pdf , (Jul 2010)

14-3 Malik H in comment to Erika Krull, When a Depresses Spouse Refuses Help, http://blogs.psychcentral.com/family/2009/06/when-a-depressed-spouse-refuses-help/, (Jun 2009)

16-1 Peggy Bert, *Positive and Negative Words Why the 5-to-1 Ratio Works*, http://www.peggybert.com/2010/09/30/positive-and-negative-words, (Sep 2009)

Patsi Krakoff, *The Magic Ratio of Positive and Negative Moments*, http://www.accomplishlife.com/articles/55/1/The-Magic-Ratio-of-Positive-and-Negative, (Dec 2004)

John Funk, M.A., *Help! Fix That Kid! How Social and Emotional Competence Encourages and Supports Healthy Behaviors*, http://www.earlychildhoodnews.com/earlychildhood/article_view.aspx?ArticleID=469

16-2 Boomerang Generation, http://en.wikipedia.org/wiki/Boomerang_Generation

16-3 *Our Adult Child is Unemployed, Living in our Basement and Drawing Heavily on our Financial Resources, What Should We Do?*, http://family.custhelp.com/app/answers/detail/a_id/25521/~/our-adult-child-is-unemployed,-living-in-our-basement-and-drawing-heavily-on, (Feb 2010)

16-4 Ibid.

16-5 Ibid.

19-1 John Gray, Ph.D., *Men are From Mars, Women are From Venus*

19-2 Dr. Tiffany Jordan, *Motivation of Employees: The Pros and Cons of What Works and Doesn't*,
http://www.businesstrainers.net/pdf/EMPLOYEE_MOTIVATION.pdf

19-3 Greg Shelley, Janssen Sports Leadership Center, *5 Keys to Motivating Your Athletes (Part 1)*,
http://www.championshipcoachesnetwork.com/public/402print.cfm

19-4 U.S. Department of Health and Human Services, Office of Women's Health, *Learning to Say "I" Instead of "You"*,
http://www.girlshealth.gov/relationships/conflict/i_statements.cfm,
(Sep 2009)

The Human Potential Center 2011, *I-Statements*,
http://www.humanpotentialcenter.org/Articles/IStatements.html,(Feb 2004)

20-1 Patricia Fry, *How to Survive Your Spouse's Job Loss*,
http://www.matilijapress.com/articles/misc_jobloss.htm, (2001)

21-1 Roswell United Methodist Church (RUMC) announcement, *Please Spread the Word* (Apr 2011)

21-2 Ruth Purple, *How to Motivate Your Husband Find a Job*,
http://www.selfgrowth.com/articles/how-to-motivate-your-husband-find-a-job

21-3 The Fox 5 Weather Authority, *Winter Weather Forecast for Atlanta*,
http://www.myfoxatlanta.com/dpp/news/local_news/winter-storm-weather-forecast-atlanta-20110108, (Jan 2011)

21-4 Jason Alba, *The Spouse's Role In Your Job Search*,
http://www.jibberjobber.com/blog/2010/01/12/the-spouses-role-in-your-job-search/, (Jan 2010)

Patricia Fry, *How to Survive Your Spouse's Job Loss*,
http://www.matilijapress.com/articles/misc_jobloss.htm, (2001)

Damsel response to post, *My Husband Lost His Job*,
http://beingfrugal.net/2008/03/27/surviving-job-loss/ (Mar 2008)

21-5 Lisa Bower, *Helping a Spouse Through Job Loss*,
http://www.life123.com/relationships/marriage/marriage-advice/helping-a-spouse-through-job-loss.shtml

21-6 Katy Abel, *When Parents Lose a Job: Talking to Kids About Layoffs*,
http://life.familyeducation.com/money-and-kids/communication/29623.html

Stephen Viscusi, *Should You Tell the Kids You Lost Your Job?*,
http://www.theladders.com/career-advice/tell-kids-lost-job , (Apr 2009)

Anita Gurian, *Talking About Job Loss with Kida – How, When and What*,
http://www.aboutourkids.org/articles/talking_about_job_loss_kids_how_when_what, (Sep 2008)

Linsey Knerl, Job Loss: What to Tell the Kids,
http://financialhighway.com/job-loss-what-to-tell-the-kids/, (May 2011)

Beth Kobliner, How to Break Bad News to Your Kids,
http://moneywatch.bnet.com/saving-money/article/bad-financial-news-how-to-tell-your-kids/312993/?tag=content;col1 ,(Jun 2009)

Roberta Rand Caponey, Coping When Your Spouse is Unemployed,
www.focusonthefamily.com/.../confronting_unemployment/coping_when_your_spouse_is_unemployed.aspx

21-7 Donna Partow, *Abiding Unemployment*,
www.focusonthefamily.com/.../life_transitions/confronting_unemployment/abiding_unemployment.aspx

21-8 Nina Chen, Helping Children Cope With a Parent's Job Loss,
http://missourifamilies.org/features/parentingarticles/parenting85.htm, (May 2009)

Patricia Fry, How to Survive Your Spouse's Job Loss,
http://www.matilijapress.com/articles/misc_jobloss.htm, (2001)

21-9 Anita Gurian, *Talking About Job Loss with Kida – How, When and What*, http://www.aboutourkids.org/articles/talking_about_job_loss_kids_h ow_when_what, (Sep 2008)

21-10 Erika Krull, When a Depresses Spouse Refuses Help, http://blogs.psychcentral.com/family/2009/06/when-a-depressed-spouse-refuses-help/, (Jun 2009)

21-11 Lisa Bower, *Helping a Spouse Through Job Loss*, http://www.life123.com/relationships/marriage/marriage-advice/helping-a-spouse-through-job-loss.shtml

Lori Fletcher, Coping with Your Husband's Job Loss, http://powertochange.com/experience/world/jobloss/

21-12 Mrs. Anita Koller, When Your Husband Loses His Job, http://www.ladiesagainstfeminism.com/artman/publish/How_to_Get _Back_Home_24/When_Your_Husband_Loses_His_Job_10081001008.sh tml, (May 2004)

suelittle29 in response to post by Frazzled, *How to respectfully tell my husband to get going on job search*, http://loveandrespect.com/forums/showthread.php?1130-How-to-respectfully-tell-my-husband-to-get-going-on-job-search,(Nov 2010)

21-13 Jason Alba, The Spouse's Role In Your Job Search, http://www.jibberjobber.com/blog/2010/01/12/the-spouses-role-in-your-job-search/, (Jan 2010)

21-14 Patricia Fry, How to Survive Your Spouse's Job Loss, http://www.matilijapress.com/articles/misc_jobloss.htm, (2001)

Focus on the Family Customer Help, *I'm suddenly unemployed; how do I tell my wife? What can I do to protect my family while I look for another job?*, http://family.custhelp.com/app/answers/detail/a_id/25752/~/i'm-suddenly-unemployed%3B-how-do-i-tell-my-wife%3F-what-can-i-do-to-protect-my, (Sep 2011)

21-15 John Gray, *Men Are From Mars, Women Are From Venus*

21-16 Roberta Rand Caponey, *Coping When Your Spouse is Unemployed*, www.focusonthefamily.com/.../confronting_unemployment/coping_w hen_your_spouse_is_unemployed.aspx

Erika Krull, When a Depresses Spouse Refuses Help,
http://blogs.psychcentral.com/family/2009/06/when-a-depressed-spouse-refuses-help/, (Jun 2009)

21-17 Kirsti A. Dyer MD, MS, FT, Caregiver Syndrome – Caregiver Stress Syndrome, http://www.squidoo.com/caregiver-syndrome

21-18 Roberta Rand Caponey, *Coping When Your Spouse is Unemployed*, www.focusonthefamily.com/.../confronting_unemployment/coping_when_your_spouse_is_unemployed.aspx

Lisa Bower, *Helping a Spouse Through Job Loss*, http://www.life123.com/relationships/marriage/marriage-advice/helping-a-spouse-through-job-loss.shtml

21-19 Lori Chidori Phillips, *Unemployment and Marriage*, http://www.bellaonline.com/articles/art4826.asp, (2011)

21-20 Nancy Mann Jackson, *How to Support Your Spouse's Job Search*, http://www.glassdoor.com/blog/support-spouses-job-search/, (Jul 2010)

22-1 Psychology Information Online, Seasonal Affective Disorder, http://www.psychologyinfo.com/depression/sad.htm

Geneva Health & Nutrition, *Vitamin D - The Amazing "Sunshine" Vitamin*, http://www.geneva-health.com/sciencehealth/sunshine.html

22-2 Erika Krull, When a Depresses Spouse Refuses Help, http://blogs.psychcentral.com/family/2009/06/when-a-depressed-spouse-refuses-help/, (Jun 2009)

22-3 Psychological Information Online, *What is a Depressive Disorder*, http://www.psychologyinfo.com/depression/description.html, *Causes of Depression*, http://www.psychologyinfo.com/depression/causes.html

Journal of Occupational Health Psychology, *Study: Depression From Job Loss is Long Lasting*, http://www.healthyplace.com/depression/workplace/study-depression-from-job-loss-is-long-lasting/menu-id-68/, (Oct 2002)

Eve Tahmincloglu, *Your Career: Reignite your job search*, http://www.nbcmiami.com/news/business/Your_Career__Reignite_y our_job_search-57658842.html, (Sep 2009)

22-4 Erika Krull, When a Depresses Spouse Refuses Help, http://blogs.psychcentral.com/family/2009/06/when-a-depressed-spouse-refuses-help/, (Jun 2009)

Index

More about Skip Freeman

And 'HeadHunter' Hiring Secrets

Today's job market is as brutal as it has ever been. In "Headhunter" Hiring Secrets, discover how to use the secrets of headhunters to turn your job search into a job found.

What makes "Headhunter" Hiring Secrets a critical component of your job hunting arsenal? You see, Skip Freeman has been in the job hunt battle every day for the last 8 ½ years. As a contingency recruiter, if he doesn't place his candidate into an open position, he doesn't eat. Thus, his methods must work and they do! He has placed over 355 people in the last 8 years with over 75 being during the recession and the post jobless recovery.

You will find that Skip's proven "headhunter" techniques will powerfully change how you think, make you adaptable, unleash your creativity and maximize all of your personal assets. You will transform yourself from just another job seeker into one who stands-out...and gets hired! Skip teaches you HOW TO PLACE YOURSELF...HOW TO RISE ABOVE YOUR COMPETITION AND WIN THE JOB YOU WANT instead of letting it go to someone else.

Skip, a distinguished graduate of the United States Military Academy, West Point, is a lifelong student of leadership, people and the principles of success. While serving in the US Army Corps of Engineers and Chemical Corps, he earned a MS degree in Organic Chemistry from The Georgia Institute of Technology and an MBA from Long Island University.

More Books by Susan Britton Whitcomb

Resume Magic

"Whitcomb has created the gold standard in resume guides." — Katherine Hansen, author of Dynamic Cover Letters, Dynamic Cover Letters for New Graduates, and A Foot in the Door: Networking Your Way into the Hidden Job Market

Filled with "before and after" resume examples that not only teach the author's special techniques but also show why they work, *Resume Magic* divulges the secrets of better resume writing from an expert with more than a decade of experience producing powerful, effective resumes.

Job Search Magic

"Any job seeker who follows the formula in this comprehensive, entertaining, and clearly written guide should expect success." — Laura A. DeCarlo, President, Career Directors International

A complete, coaching-oriented system for finding the perfect job. Includes tips on resumes, cover letters, interviews, career choice, salary negotiation.

Interview Magic

"One of the finest and definitely the most user-friendly book on interviewing that I've ever read."
— Wendy S. Enelow, CCM, MRW, JCTC, CPRW,
Author and Founder/Past President, Career Masters Institute

Interview Magic 2nd Edition is a companion to the very successful *Resume Magic* and *Cover Letter Magic*. More than an interview how-to, this "career dictionary" holds A-to-Z secrets from America's most trusted career coach. Future-proof your career as you learn to provide value to employers, create a memorable career brand, quadruple your interview opportunities, tap into the most overlooked interview "must," demonstrate your ability to do the job, and bottom-line the return-on-investment employers will receive for hiring you. In addition, identify your Achilles Heel and maintain a mindset that will increase your confidence and success.

The Christian Career Journey

Finding a new job can be an overwhelming experience. Instead of becoming flustered and losing hope, many job seekers find comfort in knowing God has a plan and a purpose for their life and career. Not only does this book reveal the seven-step process to discovering the Master F.I.T. for one's career, it offers Christ-Centered coaching questions and spirit-inspired "pocket prayers" for power and peace every step of the journey. The guide helps Christians discover the new definition of a J.O.B.-a Journey of Becoming!

30-Day Job Promotion

"The code for successfully creating a powerful job promotion plan has been broken. Its secrets are revealed in this book!"
— Perry Rhue, Certified Professional Coach and Senior Talent Manager–IBM
30-Day Job Promotion gives experienced professionals and first-time workers insider strategies for standing out and demonstrating their value to employers. These quick tips put

readers on the fast track to a promotion – and more money – in just a matter of weeks!

The Twitter Job Search Guide

This groundbreaking guide from three leading career experts will show you how Twitter can energize your job search and advance your career in just 15 minutes a day.

Join millions of users who in few characters than a standard text message have exponentially increased the size of their personal and professional networks by changing ideas, demonstrating subject matter expertise, enhancing their reputation, and developing a fan club.

About the Author

Judi Adams is the president and CEO of RightChanges.biz, the affordable and successful job search coaching company.

A 20+ year IT professional, Judi was a typical baby boomer; she thought she would retire with the same company she started with.

Judi worked for Sears for 15 years. She left Sears however to work with newer technologies. Judi worked for Hyatt Tech and Wickes Lumber before returning to the warm sunshine of Atlanta where she worked for software and consulting companies.

In her consulting capacity, Judi has worked with such diverse companies as Alagasco, AutoTrader.com, BellSouth, Byron Generating Station (Nuclear Plant), CSX Transportation, The Home Depot, Lockheed Missile and Fire Control, MEAG

Power, MidOcean Reinsurance, NASA – Kennedy Space Center, and Royal Bank of Canada.

Judi faced her first long job search in 2001 following the dot com and telecom busts, and the attacks of 9/11. From her eight month search, Judi realized how much the job market had changed. Using her passion for job seekers and her drive for process improvement, Judi created a program based upon the Crossroads Career Network program to help other job seekers leverage the knowledge she gained during her search. On a volunteer basis, Judi has shared that program with job seekers since August of 2002.

In November of 2008, Judi found herself in a career crossroads again. In February of 2009 Judi founded RightChanges.biz and has helped numerous people successfully navigate the new job market and land jobs. In fact 100% of the clients who have gone through the entire RightChanges Personal Coach Series have landed jobs they wanted; 100% !

Judi publishes job search articles that are read world-wide and has even been quoted by news agencies such as Reuters. In addition, Judi enjoys her role as a keynote speaker, giving encouragement to audiences of job seekers, career counselors, and the unhappily employed.

Along with her active work in Crossroads, Judi is an active member of International Coach Federation, Georgia Coach Association, Georgia Career Development Association, and American Business Women's Association.

Through RightChanges, Judi offers the following services:

- Personal Job Search Coaching

- Career Direct ® Career Assessment and Counseling

- Group Workshops

- Group / Corporate Outplacement Counseling

- Guest and Keynote Speaker on Numerous Topics Related to the Job Search and Interpersonal Skills

For more information, go to www.RightChanges.biz or contact Judi at Info@RightChanges.biz.

Made in the USA
Charleston, SC
18 May 2014